WITHDRAWN

French Life & Ideals

PUBLISHED ON THE FOUNDATION
ESTABLISHED IN MEMORY OF
PHILIP HAMILTON McMILLAN
OF THE CLASS OF 1894, YALE COLLEGE

This volume is based upon the series of lectures delivered at Yale University on the Bromley Foundation during the University year, 1919-1920. At that time the author was Visiting Professor and Lecturer in English Literature at Yale University.

FRENCH LIFE & IDEALS

BY

ALBERT FEUILLERAT

*Professor of English Literature in the
University of Rennes*

TRANSLATED BY VERA BARBOUR

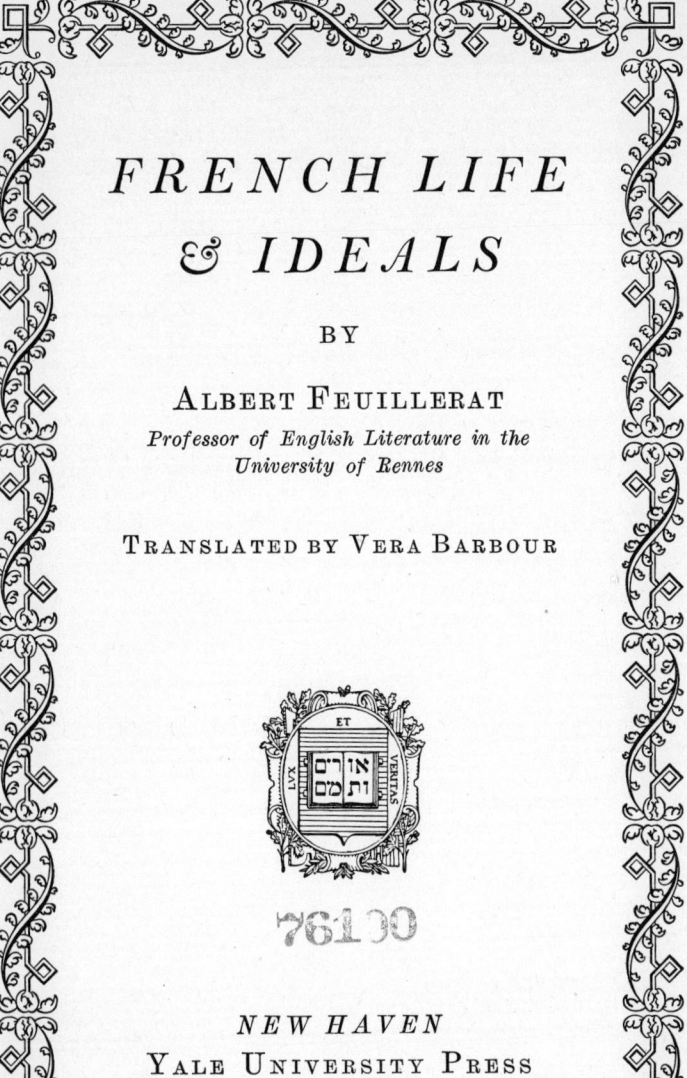

NEW HAVEN
YALE UNIVERSITY PRESS
LONDON
HUMPHREY MILFORD: OXFORD UNIVERSITY PRESS
1925

Copyright 1925 by Yale University Press
Printed in the United States of America

THE
PHILIP HAMILTON McMILLAN MEMORIAL
PUBLICATION FUND

THE present volume is the fifth work published by the Yale University Press on the Philip Hamilton McMillan Memorial Publication Fund. This Foundation was established December 12, 1922, by a gift to Yale University in pursuance of a pledge announced on Alumni University Day in February, 1922, of a fund of $100,000 bequeathed to James Thayer McMillan and Alexis Caswell Angell, as Trustees, by Mrs. Elizabeth Anderson McMillan, of Detroit, to be devoted by them to the establishment of a memorial in honor of her husband.

He was born in Detroit, Michigan, December 28, 1872, prepared for college at Phillips Academy, Andover, and was graduated from Yale in the Class of 1894. As an undergraduate he was a leader in many of the college activities of his day, and within a brief period of his graduation was called upon to assume heavy responsibilities in the management and direction of numerous business enterprises in Detroit; where he was also a Trustee of the Young Men's Christian Association and of Grace Hospital. His untimely death, from heart disease, on October 4, 1919, deprived his city of one of its leading citizens and his University of one of its most loyal sons.

Contents

I.	Formation of French Nationality	1
II.	Temperament	23
III.	Intellectual Qualities	47
IV.	Imagination	68
V.	Sentiment	91
VI.	The Social Instinct	113
VII.	Morals and Family Life	136
VIII.	Politics and Religion	160
	Notes	207

I

Formation of French Nationality

I PURPOSELY use the word "nationality," and not "race," for to-day it is admitted that no single one of the modern political groups constitutes a pure and homogeneous race. There exist only nations; that is to say, groups amalgamated in a community of language, custom, sentiment, and interest —the individuals deriving, perhaps, from quite different anthropological origins. This is particularly true of France. By its geographical situation our country was destined to become a center of attraction to all those peoples whom hunger or the predatory instinct urged forth from their frontiers. Posted at the extreme west of Europe, like a sentinel watching the limitless oceans, France is swept by the invigorating winds of the English Channel and of the North Sea; but she also feels the Mediterranean breezes—breezes warmed by the sun of the Orient— so that, one extreme of climate modifying the other, she escapes the burning heat of the African summer and the icy chill of the northern winter. Sea-bound on one half of her border, she is continental on the other half; and everywhere her land offers gently sloping hillsides and shady plains which lend themselves to tillage. France is a chosen land, where the man who wishes to escape from the uncertainties of existence is sure to find happiness and an easy life on a generous soil.

Moreover, this little promised land is wide open to all comers, not only on its shores, but also on the landward side. Indeed, one has only to glance at a map to see that "several avenues traverse central Europe from the east to the west; one, through the valley of the Danube, leads to Burgundy; another, through the Germanic plain, penetrates Picardy and Champagne; another follows as far as Flanders the alluvial littorals of the North Sea."[1] It is almost as if nature, after creating her masterpiece, had wanted to facilitate access to it.

For this reason our history is filled with the recurrent invasions which broke in waves upon our soil, leaving behind them each time a deposit of ethnic sediment. The Gauls themselves were only usurpers. In order to find the autochthonous inhabitants we must go back to prehistoric times; for our country, on account of its privileged situation, was peopled very early. At a time when Scandinavia, the chief part of Great Britain, Finland, northern Germany, and Russia from the Baltic to Kiev were but icy wastes, the plains of the future France were already inhabited.[2] And if we judge these early inhabitants by the discoveries made in the caves of Périgord, the men of the Magdalenian period had a fairly advanced civilization and even showed artistic tastes. "They understood decorative art; they had mortars for grinding colors, they had palettes and godets;[3] and the frescoes which they painted in red ochre on the walls of the grottoes show a very sure technique, a keen sense of life, and a curious custom of taking advantage of the natural irregularities of the rock-surface so as to adapt to these the representation of the animals which they were portraying."[4]

FORMATION OF FRENCH NATIONALITY

Unfortunately, we know very little about these remote ancestors of ours. We must go back thousands of years in order to see the first faint gleams of their history. According to authorities, it seems to be proved beyond doubt that before the coming of the Celts there lived over a large part, if not the whole, of Gaul, peoples which were racially allied to one another, who were called by the Greeks "Λίγυες," the Ligurians.[5] Their existence is veiled in mystery, and the only thing we can say further about them is that they were dispossessed by other more restless and more warlike tribes.

The first known invasion took place in the sixth century B.C. Toward the year 600 B.C., some Phoceans, having come by sea from the coast of Asia Minor, landed at Marseilles and founded a colony there. They were energetic traders who, after gaining a sure foothold, spread through the lower valley of the Rhone and along the Gulf of Lyons, founding other cities—Arles, Nice, Hyères, Agde.

Hardly had the Phoceans established themselves, when, from the secret fastnesses beyond the Rhine, another people appeared. They were the Celts. According to the druidic legends they came from the "far-away islands, at the world's end"[6]—without doubt, from those grassy regions which, interspersed by moors and swamps, bordered the North Sea from Jutland to Belgium.[7] They were flying from the rigor of the northern sky and seeking a milder climate. Their bands, often at enmity, followed the path traced by nature across the plains of lower Germany. Having reached the Rhine, they came into conflict with the Ligurian tribes. They succeeded, however, in crossing the river; and, going south toward the heart of the country, they stopped in what seemed to them a propitious district—that which extends between Rodez, Soissons, Saintes, and Lyons.[8]

Almost at the same time, if not earlier,[9] from an opposite quarter of the horizon another people started on the march. About 500-475 B.C.,[10] the Iberians crossed the passes of the Pyrenees and spread over the fertile plain of the southwest, occupying Béarn, Bigorre, Gers, Roussillon, and Hérault, and even pushing as far as Bordeaux.[11] They may have encountered people of their own race in this region, and they seem to have implanted themselves firmly there. It is supposed that the modern Basques are the far-off descendants of these Iberians.[11]

The success of the Celts was unquestionably the cause of a new invasion. Tribes of the same blood, known under the name "Belgians," had remained in the marshy regions of the North Sea. Moved by the same instinct which had whetted the desires of the neighboring peoples, they emigrated in their turn. Driving back the former occupants, they took possession of the country extending on both sides of the Ardennes, more particularly the valleys of the Somme, the Oise, the Aisne, and the Moselle as far as the Seine. The Belgians seem to have lived in harmony with their predecessors; indeed, they must have amalgamated with them, for the name of one of the earlier tribes, "Galates," was eventually applied to all the Celts. It was this name, under its Latin form, "Galli," which was finally used to designate our country, which thus became "Gaul."[12]

These Celto-Gallic movements lasted for about six generations. Beginning early in the fourth century

B.C., they stopped before the end of the third. One might say that this period marks the birth of a new nation. In 125 B.C. the Arverni dominated the whole of Gaul, binding together by their superior influence the majority of the other Celtic tribes, and thus making a united country of all the lands stretching from the Pyrenees and the ocean to the Rhine and the Alps. The France of the future had already found its natural frontiers.

But the Gauls did not long enjoy their triumph. A neighboring people of unbounded ambition felt the growing desire to conquer a land already coveted by so many. This time the danger came from the southeast. The Romans, since their wars with Carthage, had been in contact with all the peoples of the Mediterranean; and soon they found an opportunity to interfere in the affairs of Gaul. Called in by the Greeks of Marseilles against the Ligurians, they gained a foothold in the country about 154 B.C. A quarter of a century later they established themselves there, after organizing the Provincia Narbonensis, or, as it was sometimes called for short, "the Province"—the Provence of to-day.

It is unnecessary to recount in detail the conquest of Gaul by the Romans; the story is too well known. The Empire absorbed, little by little, all the Gallic tribes, until, having pushed its advance guard to the Rhine, it held sway over the entire country.

Under the protection of her powerful conqueror, Gaul then experienced comparative tranquillity. But with the decline of the Roman Empire she was again exposed to external attack, and the "barbarians" appeared. This was not the first time that their appetites had been whetted. A sort of fatality has always led them to covet our riches. As early as the first century of the Christian era the general Cerialis had said to the Gauls: "The same motives for invading Gaul still exist in Germania: the love of money and of pleasure, the desire for change of abode; the Germans will always be seen leaving their desolate lairs and their marshes to hurl themselves on these fertile lands of Gaul, in order to subjugate your fields and your persons."[13] Three times in succession, under the Roman rule—in 109-102 B.C., in 257 A.D., and in 275 A.D.—hordes from beyond the Rhine, Cimbri, Teutons, Franks, and Alamanni, made their way into our country, ravaging everything as they came. But each time they were defeated, and their endeavors had no other consequence than to pile ruins upon ruins. Now, however, the decaying Empire, without armies or organization, was no longer an obstacle in their path. About 406 A.D. a gathering of Germanic tribes—the Vandals and the Alani,[14] joined by some Suabians and Alamanni—crossed the Rhine between Worms and Bonn. They traversed the country without meeting any serious resistance, and Gaul knew once more the horrors of invasion. "Innumerable and ferocious hordes," writes St. Jerome in a celebrated letter, "have occupied the whole of Gaul. All the country comprised between the Alps and the Pyrenees, between the ocean and the Rhine, has been devastated by the Cuadi, the Vandals, the Sarmatians, the Alani, the Gepides, the Heruli, the Saxons, the Burgundians, the Alamanni, and the Pannonians. Mayence, formerly a famous city, has been taken and destroyed, and thousands of men have been massacred in the church. The powerful city of Rheims, the country of Amiens and of Arras, Morinia, Tournai, Spire, and Strasbourg have become Germanic. Aquitania, Novempopulania, Lugdunensis, and Narbonensis, except for a few cities, have been destroyed.'"[15]

Three states gradually emerged from these ruins. In 413 the Burgundians obtained possession of the part of Gaul near the Rhine, with the basin of the Saône, the middle valley of the Rhone, and a part of Helvetia. A little later, in 419, the Visigoths, who for a long time had been wandering across the Roman world, checked their course in southern Gaul and peopled the plains of the Garonne from Toulouse to the ocean. Finally, the Franks succeeded in establishing themselves in the north. They came from the flat countries of the lower Rhine and from the littoral of the North Sea,[16] and their incursions into Gaul had begun early. Even in 358 the Emperor Julian, in order to stop their attacks, had granted them Toxandria, the country between the Meuse and the Scheldt. From that time on, the Franks became civilized and even helped the Empire to repulse the barbarians. They established themselves by slow and continuous penetration rather than by invasion. For nearly two centuries they infiltrated, offering their services either as laborers or as soldiers. Toward the middle of the fifth century they were to be found almost everywhere in the region between the Scheldt and the Rhine, and their kingdom extended in the south as far as the territory of the Rémois. These Franks were destined to a singular fortune. They conquered the two peoples with whom they had divided Gaul, the Visigoths and the Burgundians; and it was they who gave to our country the name which she still bears—France.

Thus Gaul passed into the hands of new owners. She had not, however, seen the end of her tribulations. Toward the middle of the fifth century Attila, at the head of hordes of Tatars, Mongols, and Ural-Altaics, gathering to him Germanic marauders as he passed, crossed the Rhine between Worms and Bingen and marched against Metz. He arrived there on the sixth of April, 451, massacred the inhabitants, and burned the city. Then he swung toward the heart of Gaul, and the barbarian horde threatened Paris. At the last moment he turned aside from the capital and went straight to Orléans, which he besieged. This impulse was disastrous to him; for shortly afterward he was overwhelmed by Gallic armies massed on the Catalaunian plains in the neighborhood of Troyes—almost at the exact spot where, fifteen centuries later, General Joffre was to stem the German flood.

In the eighth century it was the turn of the Saracens. They came from Spain, where they had settled when, stimulated by the religious enthusiasm awakened by Mahomet, they had extended their Empire as far as the Atlantic Ocean. At first they occupied the south of Gaul; then, gathering together considerable forces, they went up toward the north. We find them sacking Autun on the twenty-first of August, 725. Charles Martel, then King of France, gave battle to the invaders near Poitiers and won so crushing a victory that the Arabs had to retreat to their point of departure.[17]

Then appeared the Normans. This time the invasion was by sea, from the Scandinavian countries. At first, in the reign of Charlemagne, and later, in that of Louis the Pious, their expeditions were mere

FORMATION OF FRENCH NATIONALITY

raids. But, taking advantage of the quarrels of the Carolingian princes, they grew bolder, and at the time of the battle of Fontenoy (841) we see them appearing at the mouth of the Seine, where they sacked Rouen. In 843 they pressed on as far as Nantes; other bands went up the valley of the Garonne. In 845 they were outside Paris, of which they took possession on the twenty-eighth of March. Until about 860, however, they were established on the seacoast only, whence they sallied for rapid pillaging expeditions into the interior. Their incursions into the domains of the Frankish kings and lords were continued thus for a century, until the treaty of Saint-Clair-sur-Epte (911) marked the end of their attacks. Charles the Simple, who was then King, handed over to Rollo the Dane, chief of the Norman bands, all the land comprised between the Bresle, the Epte, and the frontiers of Maine and Brittany. This state constituted the duchy of Normandy, and from that time on the Normans, implanted in the land, were part of France.

It is evidently meaningless, then, as I stated at the outset, to speak of the French race. Our nation is a compound of all the peoples who from the most ancient times have dwelt on the soil of Europe—Ligurians, Greeks, Celto-Belgians, Iberians, Latins, Cimbri, Teutons, Vandals, Alani, Suabians, Alamanni, Burgundians, Visigoths, Franks, Normans, Saracens, and the rest. And, to make the list complete, we ought to add that, even since the birth of modern France—that is to say, from the tenth century—ethnic infiltrations have continued periodically, because of the various occupations of our land by foreign armies. For it is the fate of France forever to be the debatable ground of Europe. In 1124 the German emperor, Henry V, penetrated into Lorraine and marched against Rheims. During the Middle Ages the English took possession of nearly all our maritime provinces and kept them for more than a hundred years. In the sixteenth century the emperor Charles V advanced right into Provence, Champagne, and Picardy. Philip II, in 1557, besieged St. Quentin, Ham, and Le Catelet and set fire to Noyon. In 1636 the German emperor forced the northern frontier, and the Germans slipped into France between Fourmies and Hirson, took La Capelle by storm, spread as far as the Oise, and passed the Somme, seizing Roye, Montdidier, and Corbie, pillaging and burning cities, massacring the men, violating the women, and desecrating the churches. In 1744 Hungarian and Croatian armies invaded Alsace and Lorraine. In 1815, after the defeat of Napoleon, Prussian, English, and Russian armies occupied France for more than three years. And, finally, twice during the last fifty years—in 1870 and in 1914—Germany has wanted to "colonize" France, and we have been forced to submit to the presence of her armies on our soil.

Furthermore, besides these violent penetrations we have experienced other invasions—peaceful, to be sure, but just as important in their effect on our racial mixture. More foreigners make their home in France than in any other country of Europe, whether attracted by the resources or by the pleasantness of the country. Our kings used, in olden days, to encourage these immigrations. They engaged Germans, Swiss, Hungarians, Wallachians, and Turks to reënforce their armies; they welcomed from beyond their frontiers all those who could lend a new energy to our commerce and our industry. These infiltrations continue now before our very eyes. It has been calculated that in 1911, out of a total population of 37,779,508, there were 1,159,835 foreigners. Every year a considerable number of these immigrants become naturalized; for example, 16,252 in 1912 and 17,594 in 1913. Indeed, it is no exaggeration to say that even the United States does not show more diversity of ethnic elements.

It is impossible to-day to determine the manner in which so many peoples, caught up and tossed about in the eddies of these invasions, have been amalgamated so as to form that whole which modern France has become. We can, however, inquire into the relative importance of the principal races which have taken root in our soil—Ligurian, Iberian, Celtic, Latin, and Germanic—and into what may therefore be considered as the basic elements constituting our nationality.

The part played by the Ligurians was, beyond dispute, considerable. Because their history ends in a very remote past, we sometimes forget these, our earliest ancestors. Nevertheless, the little we know about them enables us to conjecture that they were a people of great vitality, who made their influence felt far beyond their own frontiers. In the names of mountains, lakes, and springs we find words which prove how tenacious was their possession of this soil that, bit by bit, was later to be wrested from them by more warlike races.[18] Furthermore, we know that a victorious invasion never resulted in the extermination of the indigenes. Even though reduced to a dependent condition, the Ligurians must none the less have continued to occupy the country. Thus they formed the mortar on which was laid the ethnical mosaic of the successive arrivals.

The Iberian element, although of secondary importance, was not negligible. The ancients who visited the plains of the Garonne noticed the differences which distinguished the inhabitants of this region. They used to say that the Aquitanians resembled the Iberians much more than they did the Gauls. And these differences are still evident to-day: the Catalans and the Basques are recognizable by characteristics peculiar to themselves and found nowhere else in the land. They form, so to speak, an inland lake left behind by the Iberian inundation.

The part played by the Iberians cannot, however, be compared to that played by the two peoples who, coming later, were the real founders of our nationality: the Celts and the Romans. These two elements, though perhaps equal in importance, had very different formative influences. The Celts, by establishing themselves in Gaul, laid the foundations of a powerful Empire which was later to extend its sway over the greater part of Europe. It would seem that they drew a new vigor from this soil in which they had taken root. For them it was certainly the beginning of a new national existence. Possibly they had absorbed the primitive indigenous element; and their rapid propagation served, no doubt, to people the uninhabited parts of Gaul. However this may be, the imprint which they made on our country has never been effaced. The portrait of the Gauls handed down to us by Caesar bears a curious resemblance to that which we might draw of the Frenchman of to-day. Popular belief was mistaken in identifying the Gauls with the primitive race, but at bottom it was right. If the Celts were not the first occupants of the soil of France, they were at any rate the first possessors who loved that soil and who through their love created the concept of a fatherland.

The rôle of the Romans was different. Their ethnic contribution had only secondary value. Indisputably, they left behind them types which we can still recognize to-day—types so pure that sometimes, in Provence, one has the impression of seeing a procession of Roman statues come to life. But their occupation of the soil, principally military and administrative, scarcely reached farther than the southeast of France. The armies did not penetrate far beyond the frontiers, and the colonists were few in number.[19] Their intellectual contribution, on the other hand, was enormous, decisive, and transforming. To the masses of the Gauls, but lately started on the highway of civilization, the Romans opened out the treasures of an ancient past—a past which could pride itself on an incomparable literary, philosophical, and artistic production. And the conquered adopted with a surprising rapidity the customs, laws, and habits of thought of their conquerors. "To be Roman, in their eyes," said Fustel de Coulanges, "was not to obey a strange master; it was to share the manners, arts, studies, labors, and pleasures of the most cultivated and noble people known to man."[20] They were filled with so ardent an admiration that they became more Roman than the Romans. The Empire in its decline had no better defenders. Gaul became the center of Latin culture, and its writers gave renewed youth to the moribund literature of Rome. Our ancestors, out of their love for the new tongue, went so far as to forget their own. The old idiom was so completely supplanted that, of the four or five thousand primitive words of our language, scarcely one-tenth are of Celtic, Germanic, and Iberian origin. Almost all the rest are Latino-Roman. It was actually in Gaul that the purest Latin was spoken; and the conquered country gave to Rome celebrated rhetoricians and orators—L. Plotius, M. Antonius Gnipho, Vibius Gallus, Julius Florus, Votienus Montanus, Domitius Afer, Julius Africanus, Marcus Aper, Julius Secundus—as well as talented poets like Terentius Varro, Cornelius Gallus, Rutilius Claudius Namatianus, and Decimus Magnus Ausonius. Trogus Pompeius was a Gaul, as was Quintus Roscius, that actor whose reputation was so great that his name was a synonym for a man "perfect in his art."[21] One of the poets whom I have just named, Rutilius Claudius Namatianus, was justified when, at the beginning of the fifth century, he celebrated the fusion of the Gallic soul with the soul of Rome.[22]

The originality and complexity of our national temperament are due, no doubt, to the fusion of these two natures—the one, of northern origin, mobile, imaginative, and sensitive; the other, of southern origin, logical, practical, and gifted with the faculty of organization. To have harmonized so completely, the two must, fundamentally opposed though they are, have had secret affinities. Every Frenchman inherits two conflicting temperaments which seem, indeed, to be diametrically opposed, but which are amalgamated in the national character without losing their several idiosyncrasies. If the passions and sentiments of the Frenchman are, generally speaking, Celtic, his mind is preëminently Latin. It will be well to remember this distinction, for it throws light on many things.

The influence of the "barbarians" was clearly of a secondary nature. However brutal their assaults may have been, these hordes arrived too late to modify the country appreciably. These late comers were, moreover, few in number if one compares them to the peoples who for generations had been rooted in the soil. Above all, they were infinitely less civilized than those whom they happened to dominate. According to a natural law the effects of which have been often noticed, they became subservient to the superior people whom they had conquered. They were frequently content to settle alongside the Gallo-Romans, adopting their administration, customs, religion, and even language. This is the best proof that, far from having fashioned the country in their own image, they submissively learned lessons from it, in the end, doubtless, allowing themselves to be entirely absorbed.

It is a long time now since the fusion of all these elements was completed: yet the traces of the different ethnic contributions are still visible. The anthropologists recognize the presence of four races in France: "(1) a dark type, dolichocephalous and of small stature, in Angoumois, Limousin, and Périgord; (2) a dark type, very brachycephalous and of small stature, in the Cevennes, the Plateau Central, the Alps, Brittany (with the exception of Morbihan), Poitou, and Quercy; (3) a dark type, mesocephalous and of tall stature, on the coast of the Mediterranean and the Gulf of Gascony and in the lower valley of the Loire; and (4) a dark type, brachycephalous and of tall stature, between the Loire and the Saône, on the plateau of Langres, in the Ardennes, and in the upper valleys of the Saône and the Moselle (one finds it also, somewhat attenuated, in the middle basin of the Loire, and, somewhat smaller and less brachycephalous, in Perche, Champagne, the Vosges, Franche-Comté, and Lorraine).''[23] In other words, whereas most nations are composed of two races only,[24] one finds in France the three ethnic types recognized in Europe and even traces of a prehistoric people which has disappeared almost everywhere else.

As a fact, this classification gives only a very imperfect idea of the varieties of men to be found on the soil of France. The ethnic groups which resulted from the fluxes and refluxes of so many peoples, and from the interbreeding which was the inevitable consequence, are incalculably more numerous than anthropology gives us to understand. An observer traveling in our country cannot fail to be struck by the dissimilarities that distinguish the inhabitants when he passes from one to another of the great natural regions which correspond to our old provinces. And these dissimilarities create an equal number of characteristic types, recognizable not only by the peculiarities of stature, color of hair and eyes, shape of head, pigmentation of the skin, but also by the gait, the tones of the voice, the bearing—in short, by an ensemble of attitudes and gestures; an ensemble which, although almost indefinable, makes the trained observer say at once, when he sees a Frenchman, ''You are a Provençal''—or a Norman,

FORMATION OF FRENCH NATIONALITY

Lorrainer, Breton, Alsatian, Fleming, Morvandiau, Auvergnat, or Franc-Comtois, as the case may be.

We are indisputably, then, a mixture of diverse races. Yet we have only to ignore the somatic characteristics and consider the customs and manners of thinking and feeling, to see the differences magically disappear and become merged in a single national type, amazingly unified. The blood of ten peoples flows in our veins: yet no nation presents a more perfect homogeneity. There are twenty kinds of Frenchmen; but—so true is it that, by a sort of miracle, all our component elements have fused to form a harmonious and indissoluble whole—in essentials of the mind and spirit all Frenchmen are alike.

This phenomenon has several causes. The first must be sought in the dangers which have always menaced France. The invasions which are the cause of our diversity have also, by a curious turn of things, helped to create our unity. There is nothing like misfortune for drawing men together. "Common suffering," said Renan, "has a more unifying power than joy. As national memories, disasters are of more value than triumphs; for they impose duties—they demand a common effort."[25] Constantly attacked, the victim of at least one invasion in every century, France needed, if she were to defend herself, to draw the ranks of her sons closely together. And in these great gatherings she acquired her national consciousness very early—long before any other European nation. In all these battalions which flocked together from every part of her territory,

17

their individual traits lost in the mêlée, there appeared, first faintly and then ever more clearly, her own image.

Environment has also played its part in this intermixture of disparities. Without wishing to give this influence an undue value, we must recognize that the well-known or obscure forces of nature that surround us influence the formation of our temperament, and hence our entire being. Now, the land of France has a very marked identity. Strongly defined by her natural frontiers, she seems to have been destined to constitute a whole very distinct from the rest of Europe. She was a physical entity before being a political entity. And, leading to the very heart of her territory, nature has laid a network of paths that invite communication. The entrances to her river basins, which have been compared to three cradles of races, are of easy access and have facilitated intercourse. From the earliest times there has been an enormous traffic on the highways of France,[26] mingling the men of the different provinces. Let us add that, in this compact land, one breathes the same air everywhere. In vain do geographers distinguish as many as seven climates within the small area of our country; they all have one characteristic in common: the absence of extremes. The traveler who, crossing France, starts from the north in order to reach the south—as he can easily do in little more than a day—will have no such impression of entering a new world as is experienced by the man, who, for example, goes without stopping from New Orleans to Chicago. Everywhere there floats the same equable and temperate atmosphere; and its action is all the more powerful because it affects one unconsciously. Consistently mild, the negation of excess, it influences everything and everybody. It obliterates dissimilarities; it softens contradictions and subdues them into charming half-tones, interpenetrating every gradation like that pearly-gray tone which, as painters know, constitutes the fundamental coloring of all French landscape. It is almost impossible to resist an influence so continuous and so magical. It has been often remarked that France absorbs and transforms, with a marvellous rapidity, all that she receives. "There contrasts fade away; invasions languish. It would seem that there is something about her that softens angles and mellows contours."[27] Foreigners, even those belonging to the most refractory races, are so thoroughly assimilated in a few years that it is often impossible to distinguish them from their new compatriots. It is not rare to see Frenchmen by adoption identify themselves completely with their new country and adore it more unreservedly than do the French themselves. The Corsican Napoleon and the Italian Gambetta are striking examples.

But, even more than these causes, what has contributed preëminently to the unification of France is the persistence of a certain political and social ideal, envisaged from the time when the nation became conscious of its unique physical position, and pursued with incredible tenacity through the centuries. As early as the fifth century we see born in the heart of Clovis the idea that France, by virtue of her very topography, was destined to form one great people; and, with this clear vision of the future, the Frankish king worked to unite under the same law the scattered and turbulent elements which at that time dwelt in Gaul. It was toward this ideal that all our kings tended. Through many deviations—and through many errors, too—we can follow their persevering efforts to break the resistance of undisciplined vassals and to lead them to abdicate their power in favor of a single more powerful authority. In the twelfth century, when Germany was vegetating in a state of rudimentary existence, France was already a moral entity to whom all her sons rendered homage and affection. Even during the reign of the Valois, whose faults often endangered the work begun, the consolidation continued, to reach its perfection under the Bourbons. At that time France arrived at her apogee; and never, perhaps, has her splendor been brighter or more beneficent. She acquired her geographical frontiers from the Pyrenees to the Rhine, and everywhere her name was a synonym for civilization. The revolutionary period, even if it overthrew the social and political state, safeguarded this ideal; nay, revolutionary France made it her own, and the unification of the country remained more than ever the directing thought of all the successive governments. When Napoleon arrived in his turn, it only remained for him, with a blow of his heavy hammer, to rivet the centralization of power which had been the goal of all his predecessors, as it still is the living principle of our whole political and administrative organization.

To-day the unification is complete, and all the elements which have entered into the composition of France are so closely bound together that nothing can ever again force them apart. This truth became evident when our country was brutally attacked in

August, 1914. At France's cry of distress the whole nation rose, determined to defend to the death the moral heritage which had been slowly garnered for centuries. Provinces, classes, existed no longer. Provençals and Lorrainers, Bretons and Gascons, Flemings and Basques, rich and poor, capitalists and socialists, all had but one idea: to save the land of which each one felt that he formed an inalienable part. The Germans, with that incredible ignorance of psychology which explains all their political mistakes, were counting on our disunion in order to get the better of us. If they had known history as they flattered themselves that they did, they might have read in our past the wonderful record of the formation of French unity; and then they would have understood that that which had been realized by an effort of fourteen centuries could not be undone by the menace of a few hours.

It is this history, as stirring as an epic poem, which I have tried to tell you to-day—of necessity, very briefly. This résumé will enable you at least to understand why the Frenchman is both one and many, both simple and complex. Because he is one, we can endeavor to sketch a general likeness of him. But, having absorbed all that was assimilable from the other peoples, he is a compound of instincts, sentiments, qualities, and faults which sometimes accord with and complete, sometimes antagonize and contradict, one another. The most French of Frenchmen is never himself alone. Sometimes he shows us one side and sometimes another, according to circumstances. The reason is that, as occasion prompts, there arises from the troubled depths of his being this or that one of his diverse heredities. It is obviously not easy to explain a being made up of contradictions; and France has rightly been called the Sphinx of Europe. Let us see, however, if it is not possible to force the Sphinx to tell us her riddle.

II

Temperament

I AM going to begin the psychological study of the Frenchman by analyzing that which lies at the very root of his being: that is to say, his temperament. I use the word in its ordinary acceptation and with the broadest meaning. I mean by temperament that irreducible part of ourselves which results from all the characteristics transmitted to us from our different ancestors—a common heritage of qualities or faults which we receive at birth, independently of what education and conscious will may later add to these predispositions.

It is the manifestations of the national temperament which foreigners especially notice. Very often these manifestations are the only things they do remark; and I am tempted to add that they are the things which foreign observers understand least in connection with the Frenchman. If I were to choose at random ten persons in this room and were to ask each of them, "What are the most striking traits of the French character?" I am quite sure that nine of them would answer unhesitatingly, "Levity, frivolity, and inconstancy"; and the tenth, if he hesitated, would probably be thinking that the others were right. Such is, in fact, the current opinion about the French. It is an opinion which, at any rate, has antiquity to recommend it. We find it formulated as early as the sixteenth century, and

I am very much afraid that Shakespeare helped crystallize it and spread it. You remember the portrait which Portia drew of the French suitor: it is not flattering. Later the idea spread and became amplified. It took cruel forms when we and the English were not on good terms; it became merely bantering under the pen of writers who were sympathetic to us—*e.g.,* Cowper when he said in his *Table Talk:*

> The Frenchman, easy, debonair, and brisk,
> Give him his lass, his fiddle, and his frisk,
> Is always happy, reign whoever may,
> And laughs the sense of misery far away.

And the English have not been the only ones to misjudge us. The Americans—as Fenimore Cooper, in his *Recollections of Europe,* remarks and regrets—have too often adopted without modification this foreign opinion. I could give you proofs. But what is the good? Such is the world. To the majority of people the Frenchman is an unstable creature, careless, frivolous, changeable, and so on. I leave it to you to complete the list of the synonyms which one can easily gather around this idea.

Without doubt there is a modicum of truth in this opinion; none of the judgments made by one people upon another is radically false. But such generalizations are obviously superficial. Foreigners see only one side, the outer, of the tissue of actions; they are ignorant of the inner side, which, if it were better known, would modify, correct, or even reverse their first impression. Above all, they do not sound the reasons for the faults on which they seize, and thus they obscure the true significance of those faults and their relative importance in the temperament as a whole. Let us, before we attempt to correct the picture, see to what extent their observation is correct.

It is certain that our people, by reason of its descent, is at once sanguine-nervous—the inheritance from its northern ancestors—and neuro-bilious, the inheritance from its southern ancestors. From this combination of two opposite temperaments— which, however, have one character in common— there has resulted a hyper-tonicity of the nervous system, exaggerated still further in the south of France by climatic action.[1] For this reason we are particularly impressionable. We still answer, up to a certain point, to the description of the Gauls given by Polybius and Strabo. People speak at a higher pitch and more rapidly in our country than in countries where sensibility is less acute. They even shout, jostle one another, dispute over a mere nothing. It is astonishing to see how life, especially in Paris, offers opportunities for scolding. The maid-servant who does her work too slowly, a debatable point in a game of cards between old cronies, a lack of respect to a tyrannical concierge, too protracted a wait in a post-office—a thousand trifles of this sort are material for vocal outbursts and general excitement.

Because the nervous tempo of our being is very rapid, we are capable of impulsive, sudden, and almost explosive actions. We are easily set on fire by an idea, a cause; we abandon ourselves utterly to a spirit of exaltation that carries us away and prevents us from seeing the obstacles in our path. And, as happens with enthusiasms not supported by reflection, these ardors cannot long be sustained at the same pitch. When the reaction comes, the result is depression; and this may even have the appearance of discouragement, although it represents simply a return to the normal state which we ought not to have left. We seem to have acted giddily and heedlessly; and thus we lay ourselves open to the reproach of instability.

We are, moreover, the most optimistic people in the world; it is the nature of the sanguine temperament. And this predisposition has been further intensified by the conditions of our existence. In a climate which does not provoke violent physical reactions, man is led to see life in its most smiling aspect. The present is full of charm; the past, therefore, is quickly forgotten, and the future holds no menace. "Sufficient unto the day is the evil thereof" is a proverb which you will often hear from our lips. If to-day is favorable, why should to-morrow be less so? If difficulties arise, there will always be time to take thought. Whoever wants to can always "get out of it." Let us enjoy life, then, its goodness and its bounty. Let us extract from it all that it can give us. It is generous and full of miracles. A mere nothing can contain an immensity of enjoyment. A crowd, a dispute, some laborers working on the public highway, a "gotha" which is trying to launch its devastating bombs—any such thing is a subject for interest; and if evil too often treads upon the heels of good, that only proves that good is never far from evil. A ray of the sun struggling to pierce a screen of cloud on a gray day is enough to restore a Frenchman to good temper.

For it is certainly to our optimism that we owe our gayety. This is an essentially French character-

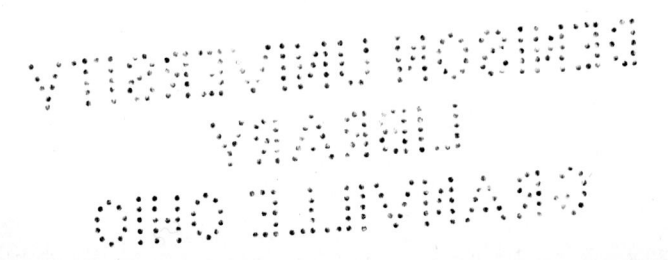

TEMPERAMENT

istic, or at any rate it is the most striking and essential manifestation of our temperamental exuberance. Very early, France was the country of good humor. Was it not Rabelais who asserted that *"Le rire est le propre de l'homme"?*—that laughter is the distinguishing quality of man? Our ancestors did not hesitate to make a generous use of this privilege of being human by driving care away with merry jests. A very old poet said:

>*Les rois, les princes, les courteurs,*
>*Comtes, barons, et vavasseurs,*
>*Aiment contes, chansons, et fables*
>*Et bons dits qui sont délitables,*
>*Car ils ôtent le noir penser;*
>*Deuil et ennui font oublier.*

>Lords and nobles, knights and kings,
>Barons, landed princelings,
>Joy in tale and song and fable,
>Hold that mirth is profitable.
>Such things put to rout dull care,
>Banish tedium or despair.

And this belief has been transmitted to us piously from century to century. Even under Louis XIV, notwithstanding the formality of the period, gayety did not cease to be a virtue. Mme. de Sevigné could find no greater praise to give of M. de Coulanges, whom she much admired, than to say that "gayety made a great part of his merit,"[2] and that "the style in which one writes to him is like happiness and health."[3] A little later the author of *L'Esprit des Lois* opposed eagerly those who wished to reform the character of the Frenchman: "If there existed anywhere a nation which had a sociable humor, open-heartedness, joy of living, taste, and a facility in communicating its thoughts; which was vivacious, agreeable, gay, sometimes imprudent, often indiscreet; and which, in addition, had courage, generosity, and frankness, and was sensitive about honor, one should not try to restrain its manners by law, for fear of restraining its virtues. . . . If one enforces a pedantic spirit upon a naturally gay nation, the state will gain nothing by it.'"[4]

But why search our literature for proofs of the commonness of this national trait? To look around one is enough. Watch any Frenchman in the street. If he is in his normal condition, you will certainly not see on his face the tenseness of features, rigidity of the lips, and sternness of glance habitual to other peoples who are of cold temperament or who wish to seem aloof and superior. You will see an expression of intimate satisfaction and ease on his face, a smile on his lips, and a light of contentment in his eye, as if he were secretly conversing with an invisible and particularly charming person. Should he meet a friend, it is a thousand to one that the vague smile on his lips will expand. Our man will accost this friend with some joke or witticism, and the conversation will be continued in the same gay vein until, with a burst of laughter, they separate. And that is why the French street is so animated, so noisy, and so tonic. "There is something in the air of France that carries off the blue devils!" said Hazlitt.[5]

This spontaneous, expansive, and persistent gayety may, I admit, appear like incurable carelessness when one considers it from the outside, as a mere spectator, without participating in it or trying

TEMPERAMENT

to penetrate its peculiar quality. But he who knows the sources from which it springs sees instantly that to find in it a proof of frivolity is to misunderstand it. First of all, it has its origin, as we have seen, in a certain power of enjoying life indefatigably and to the full. Now this happy disposition, if one will only reflect upon it, is a somewhat rare gift. One is not an optimist at will. Our nature may lead us to see everything in a rosy light, but we shall maintain this condition only if our mind is ready to resist the whims of fate. To take life as it comes, courageously to accept its buffetings, one must have good sense and moderation, the privilege of none but those who know how to judge the world in which we live. This presupposes a happy equilibrium of all the faculties, a sort of constant serenity. It is, in the truest sense, a proof of wisdom.

Besides, you must remember that this gayety is far from being a sign of simplicity. Precisely because it rests on a foundation of experience, it is more than the response to a mere need for agreeable impressions. The Frenchman does not laugh at everything or on every occasion. Indeed, he is particularly exacting in the choice of the subjects or objects by which he consents to be diverted. He may even be bored on occasions when other peoples, who pass as grave, will be hugely amused. How many times have I heard certain compatriots of mine mutter, "It isn't funny," when they heard a joke which, although it made foreigners go into paroxysms of mirth, they considered childish. The fact is that, in our eyes, gayety must have to recommend it a certain depth, a basis of intellectual significance. We wish to be amused, but not without good reason.

It is out of the ludicrous aspects of life that we extract our amusement. The Frenchman's laughter is never far from irony, and it easily turns to satire.

The satirical spirit is no less inherent in our nature than gayety itself. In truth, the two are inseparable. Look at our popular songs. There are few, even among the amorous complaints, which do not have a comic or mocking note. Almost always they are parodies, like *Cadet Rouselle* or that *Malbrough s'en va-t-en guerre* which has been and still is the cradle-song of so many French children. This mocking spirit appears in the very dawn of our literature. This spirit it was which, contemporaneously with the *Chanson de Roland,* that idealized picture of the Carolingian epoch, gave rise to the contrasting *Pélerinage de Charlemagne* and to the numerous caricatures of the great emperor. It is strongly shown in the *Roman de Renard* and in our *fabliaux;* and from that time on, it never ceased to sharpen the pens of our authors. It appears preëminently in satire properly so called—the philosophical satire of Rabelais and his successors. It appears in the political satire of the Ménippée, in the social satires of Boileau and of La Bruyère. It triumphs like an all-devouring fire in our brilliant comedy— the mode in which we excel, for comedy is, of all the genres, the one which best allows the union of gayety with the critical faculty. Finally, it is this same satirical spirit, a little modified, which gives a special flavor to the most essentially French masterpieces—those of Montaigne, La Fontaine, Voltaire, Daudet, and Anatole France.

When this jesting spirit is given free play for the simple pleasure of indulging it and on occasions when it is out of place, it takes the rather disagreeable form which we call *blague*. This is more especially a Parisian idiosyncrasy, but a very French one nevertheless. It consists primarily in pretending not to take seriously what one actually respects—in hiding the most sincere convictions under an appearance of cynicism, in ridiculing what in one's heart one considers sacred, in steeling oneself against emotion and tenderness. It is a rather irritating attitude, yet a quite inoffensive one; for it does not affect the deep sources of feeling. But in the eyes of foreigners who are ignorant of its peculiar significance it takes on an exaggerated importance and causes to be imputed to us a good many faults which we do not really have. *Blague* is, of all French traits, the one that has probably been our worst enemy.

On the other hand, when our satirical spirit is turned to good account it can exert an eminently beneficial influence. A French proverb has it that ridicule kills. Ridicule has, in fact, killed many prejudices and abuses in our country. The French Revolution was started by bursts of laughter. Beaumarchais helped the birth of a new order by ridiculing on the stage the privileged classes of his time. And so powerful is the sway of gayety over the French spirit that the very people who had been attacked greeted with enthusiastic applause the satires directed against them. The memoirs of the time have preserved for us the recollections of the extraordinary success of the first performances of *Le mariage de Figaro*—"the public besieging the theater, the noblemen mixed with the crowd and waiting in line with porters and lackeys, great ladies dining in the actresses' boxes so as to be sure of their seats two hours beforehand."[6]

French gayety often has, then, a morally civilizing force which shows that, far from being a sign of frivolity, it is quite likely to be associated with the most serious intentions. By an extension which amounts almost to a reversal of its nature, it can even denote actual nobility of soul. Our history abounds in examples of laughter become the sign of a sort of stoicism, repressed, to be sure, but for that very reason the more admirable. For example, Molière, seized by a convulsion in the middle of *Le Malade Imaginaire*, forced himself to hide his overwhelming agony under witticisms, thereby justifying a remark which Madame Dupin de Francueil made to her granddaughter, George Sand. "In old days," she said, "people knew how to live and how to die. They had no importunate infirmities; a man would have had himself carried to a hunting party when he was half dead. People enjoyed life, and when the hour came to lose it they did not do their best to make life repulsive to everybody else."[7]

And there was Scarron, who bore with unalterable good humor both financial distress and the unspeakable sufferings of an incurable malady that racked his limbs. In the midst of his tortures, crippled, seemingly doomed to a quite excusable melancholy, he was actually able to keep on reeling off his audacious little verses—verses sparkling with malice under the sometimes rather facile vulgarity of their clowning. He could not even forego joking about his own miseries, and a short time before his death he wrote this epitaph on himself:

TEMPERAMENT

Celui qui cy maintenant dort
Fit plus de pitié que d'envie,
Et souffrit mille fois la mort
Avant que de perdre la vie.
Passant ne fais icy de bruit:
Garde bien que tu ne l'éveille:
Car voici la première nuit
Que le pauvre Scarron sommeille.

A thousand times he suffered death
   —He who sleeps beneath this stone—
Before he drew his parting breath.
   Him many pitied; envied none.
Respect the silence that he keeps.
   Be quiet here, thou passing wight!
For, look thou, poor old Scarron sleeps,
   Who never slept until to-night.

Do you not think that there is something more than incorrigible mockery in these verses which so strangely stir our sympathy?

And consider the Emigrés at the time of the Revolution. Suddenly thrown down from the heights of power and wealth, they found themselves living from hand to mouth. They had to earn their own livelihood, and they were scarcely prepared for it. Did they complain? Indeed, no: that would not have been like Frenchmen. They did not give up their title to gayety; and since they could not avert misfortune, they laughed at it. They worked by day, and by night they gathered together and acted plays. Some of them said charming things. The Comtesse de Neuilly, who kept a shop at Hamburg, exclaimed one evening as she was getting ready for a party: "At last I am going to play a little at being a lady;

I have been a shopkeeper all day."[8] Is that frivolity? No, certainly not; it is purest courage—the courage which shows itself naturally, without ostentation; the hardest courage of all, because it can never be rewarded by public recognition. It is a form of unconscious stoicism. It is the same kind of courage which brought jokes to the lips of the Chevalier de La Barre on the eve of his execution,[9] and which prompted Danton to a witticism at the moment when he laid his head under the guillotine.

We have seen that same courageous smile, finer than ever, irradiating and, as it were, dazzling human agony in the recent war. The years preceding hostilities brought forth one expression which had a great vogue. Of persons who showed a serene front in difficult or precarious circumstances, it was said that they "had the smile." These words took on a very poignant meaning during the great struggle from which we have now emerged. During the four long years in which she lived in sorrow and anguish, all France "had the smile." Listen to this letter by a young soldier who was killed shortly after writing it. He was barely twenty; he still called his mother "Maman"! Here are his thoughts in the midst of peril: "My poor Maman, I am between two hedges, and the balls are whistling behind my head. I am saying goodbye to you. Perhaps I shall not see you again. . . . I am gay. . . . I sing all the time. . . . I shall sing till the end."[10] And here is a passage from the letter of a young officer killed October 6, 1915: "I am living the best day of my life. I regret nothing, and I am as happy as a King. I am happy to be killed so that my country may be delivered. Tell all the dear ones that I am going to victory with

TEMPERAMENT

a smile on my lips, more joyful than all the stoics and martyrs of all time. We are one moment of Eternal France. France must live, France shall live. Prepare your beautiful dresses. Keep your smiles to greet the victors of the Great War. We shall perhaps not be there; others will be there for us. You will not weep. You will not wear mourning for us, for we shall have died with a smile on our lips and a superhuman joy in our hearts.'"[11] That is how, during the war, the children of France died. They did not fall with a threat in their eyes and their teeth clenched in hate: they left us singing, with a smile on their lips. And at home it was the same. There, too, one wanted to "have the smile"—in public, at least; for when one was alone with one's thoughts, behind closed doors, it was often another story.

This was not always very well understood by strangers. They came to our country; they saw people who had forced themselves to adopt a certain attitude, and who joked and laughed—in order not to give way to tears. And then the old accusation of frivolity was born again in their minds. I will relate to you a story of which the dramatis personæ are known to me, and which will enable you to realize the extent of this misunderstanding. A young woman had lost her husband during the great assault against Verdun. He had been swept away like a straw by the enemy's artillery. Nobody could say what had become of his body. They were a very united couple, and the blow, I know, must have been heavy. But she was valiant, and she made it a point of honor not to be crushed. She went on with her former life, suffering nothing to be changed. One day one of her English friends went to see her—a man who had known her as a little girl, and who loved her as his own daughter. What was his astonishment to find Marguerite—that was her name—just as he had known her before, bright, charming, vivacious. He could not believe his eyes. With that sentimentalism which is at the root of the English character, he refused to admit that such a sorrow ought not to be accompanied by a face of gloom, indelibly marked with grief. He unburdened his heart to me. "I don't understand Marguerite," he said. "Before, she was tender, sensitive almost to excess. And here she is, seeming hardly to notice the death of her husband." I tried to explain to him that, according to one of our sayings, great sorrows are mute. He was obstinate in his disillusionment. One evening he came rushing to me, absolutely overwhelmed. This time he was convinced. He had gone to call unexpectedly. He had knocked at the door of the room in which his friend habitually sat. Nobody having answered his knock, he had gone in; and there he had found the young woman, on her knees, with bowed head, sobbing bitterly.

I have said that foreigners do not always understand us. There are some, however, who have done us justice; notably, a Spanish writer, Gomez Carillo, who, indeed, has analyzed our character so perfectly that I ask your permission to quote his words. "Those who know only Paris, with its perpetual fever and unrest, have not the faintest conception of the real French gayety, ingenuous, sprightly, light, gallant, fresh, loquacious, healthy, and robust as it is. 'Gallic laughter,' say foreigners. I prefer to call it Athenian, so subtle is it and so

TEMPERAMENT

full of those delicate nuances which one finds so astonishing in the common people and so much more astonishing in the people under arms and at war. . . . But for this superficial frivolity how could the France of yesterday and to-day have borne the misfortunes heaped upon her by fate? By laughing and singing she has always managed to escape the prostration into which grave peoples, such as the Spaniards and the Turks, fall as soon as they feel that they have met with defeat. Ah, if poor France had not kept her laughter in 1870! But those who do not see what depth, what seriousness, and, one might almost say, what piety there is under this frivolity, do not know the soul of the country. To march to death singing and jesting is to sanctify frivolity."[12]

That is going to the root of things. Gomez Carillo saw that French gayety may mask serious thoughts without destroying them. The same author relates another anecdote which will enable me to elaborate this point. In his book entitled *Au cœur de la Tragédie,* in which he described his experiences on the British front, he relates how he once expressed his astonishment at seeing the English soldier so taciturn; and the officer who was accompanying him cried out quickly: "Our people are serious, no doubt, but this seriousness is more external than internal. I hate to say it, but we have something of the gravity of the clown, who, after having walked around the circus, turns a somersault, bursts out laughing, runs after a dog, and then at last goes and sits down in an armchair as if nothing mattered to him"[13]—a remark which throws light on the essential difference between the French and the English temperaments. In similar circumstances the two peoples comport themselves in diametrically opposite ways. The Englishman purposely hides his gayety under imperturbable seriousness; to a Frenchman, gayety is often a mask beneath which his seriousness is concealed.

Seriousness is, in truth, a very French quality. Because it is always hidden under gayety, it is more difficult to detect. But it forms an essential part of our temperament, of which it is, so to speak, the bed rock; and those foreigners who have understood us best have not failed to recognize this fact. Bacon, whose perspicacity is unquestionable, stated that the French are graver than they seem.[14] Sterne went farther. Inclosing a truth in a paradox, as was his wont, he said: "If the French have a fault, it is that of being too serious."[15] One of your own writers, Fenimore Cooper, also did us justice when he said: "Two capital mistakes exist in America on the subject of France. One regards its manners. . . . We believe that French deportment is superficial, full of action, and exaggerated. That would truly be a wonder in a people who possess a better tone of manners, perhaps, than any other; for quiet and simplicity are indispensable to high breeding."[16]

I could lengthen the list of witnesses; but I will be content to add the testimony of one more of your compatriots—one who is not far from thinking, as Sterne did, that we are grave to excess. I mean the late Barrett Wendell, formerly a professor at Harvard, and certainly one of the most penetrating of the foreigners who have written about France.

When Mr. Wendell left America in 1904 to take up the duties of exchange professor at the Sorbonne, he set out, I imagine, with all the foreigner's

TEMPERAMENT

typical ideas about France. He expected to find a polite, amiable, and sympathetic people, but one which would give his Boston seriousness a severe trial. And what was his surprise to have to admit from the very first that, in the society in which he moved, where he had expected to encounter a people greedy for amusement, an immense industry was the rule. He could not resist showing his admiration. But I will let him speak for himself: "On the surface, perhaps, the French still preserve something of the gayety which has made foreigners suppose them to be agreeably frivolous. When you grow to know them, at least among the bourgeoisie this characteristic is no longer salient. Rather you find yourself constantly surprised that so many people, with honest simplicity of heart, can devote themselves so assiduously to the far from alluring duties—professional, domestic, or whatever else—of daily, weekly, yearly existence. However gay a friend may be concerning trivial matters, you may be sure that, at heart, he will take life in earnest; and that when it comes to hard work, he will attack it with a persistent vigor which might sometimes set a Yankee to wondering whether our lucky compatriots have any notion of how lovingly we cherish our national aptitude for dawdling. I do not remember that I ever saw a French boy whittle a stick; I doubt whether you could quite make one understand why anybody should like to."[17]

Elsewhere, Mr. Wendell speaks of the conscientiousness which professors and students show in their work: "None of my previous experience had revealed to me anything like such a spectacle of concentrated and increasing intellectual activity as seemed a matter of course among my temporary colleagues at Paris. Foreign prejudice is apt to suppose the French lighthearted, frivolous, and at best superficial. When you live among French men of learning engaged in the work of their lives you begin to wonder whence this grotesque misconception arose. For nobody could imagine industry more unremitting than theirs, and, for all its cheerfulness, more intense.'"[18]

This love of work, which Mr. Wendell was enabled to observe among the intellectuals, animates all the classes of society. It is still the predominating quality of the French workman. Even the theories (of foreign origin) about the limitation of the hours which the workman owes his master, if they have somewhat dimmed this ancient and solid virtue, have not been able to destroy it. How often one sees workmen, their day's work done, undertaking some supplementary job in order to add a little to their daily wage! This love of work sustains also the numerous class of small commercial employés, who often toil with untiring cheerfulness from ten to twelve hours a day, sometimes for ridiculous salaries, and who, by prodigies of ingenuity, manage to make both ends meet, bring up their children well, and even maintain a prosperous appearance. And, finally, you will see this love of work among our peasants, from north to south, from east to west. Wonderful peasant stock! I do not believe that there is any in the world like it. Of course, the French peasant has his faults; do I not know them? His love for the soil is so great that it often fills his heart to the point of absorbing every other sentiment. He has also, at any rate in certain parts of France, too marked a love of the bottle; we have too many Falstaffs in certain of our country districts. But what do these weaknesses matter, compared with the patient energy of which the peasant gives constant proof? With what ardor he devotes himself to his daily task! Rising at cockcrow, prolonging his day long after the shadows cast by the sun fade into the gray-blue of twilight, he never balks at work. The more work the French peasant has, the happier he is. It is not he who hankers after the eight-hour day—the six-hour day —whatever it may be. If he could make his voice heard in heavenly affairs, he would rather pray God to suspend time, so that he might be the better able to satisfy that lust for work which is his ideal and his faith. The peasant represents in France, in a simple and rather primitive form, those qualities of untiring vigor and assiduity in labor which so powerfully impressed Mr. Wendell.

Perhaps it is the old Ligurian foundation which thus persists under us. Those earliest ancestors of ours belonged, as our peasants belong to-day, to a robust race of extraordinary resistance—a race sturdy in toil. They were courageous and hardworking. They were also, it would seem, fond of gain—another French characteristic. Our habit of economy is indeed proverbial; it is often cited against us as a fault. It is possible that some French people push the love of money to an extreme: avarice is a human weakness, and Frenchmen are men. But I deny that this vice is general, or even very common, in our country. When we happen to notice it, it revolts us. The man who loves money for money's sake seems to us despicable, and we despise him. Do not forget that two of the most pitiless satires against avarice which exist—Molière's *L'Avare* and Balzac's *Eugénie Grandet*—are French works. In reality there is no man more generous than the Frenchman. From the earliest times prodigality has passed among us for a sign of nobility. "The better born one is," said Luchaire, speaking of the Middle Ages, "the more one should give to friends, to vassals, to players, to all comers."[119] Incontrovertible proofs of this taste for expenditure have been left in those rich dwellings the artistic beauty and luxury of which are the admiration of foreigners. And, even to-day, are not Frenchmen notorious for the excessive liberality with which they distribute tips? This generosity is, in truth, a natural effect of their optimism, which leads them, when they follow their instinct, to have no fear for the morrow. But, by one of those contradictions which prove that there are in us always two conflicting temperaments, we have an invincible horror of waste. We wish our expenditure to be rightly proportioned to our needs; we particularly insist that it should give us the maximum of pleasure or comfort. To live economically is what Béranger used to call "squandering less and enjoying more." We see it as a question of common sense, and also of force of character. To indulge all one's fancies, to spend money as quickly as one earns it—is not that a proof that one does not know how to resist the impulses of instinct? The economical man is rather he who, as Mr. William Archer says, knows how to restrain his first impulses.[20] To administer one's fortune wisely and with judgment, to know how to refuse oneself useless pleasures, presupposes a great self-mastery, and, far from being a fault, is

TEMPERAMENT

a proof of will power and firmness. It is another manifestation of that latent energy which may be dissimulated under each of our actions.

And here we come to another of the French qualities which have been very often misunderstood—energy. Certainly, it is not so often revealed in commercial competition as it ought to be. But it exists, nevertheless, and it answers our call when occasion demands. Those who know our history cannot deny this. It is this quality which explains that prodigious power of recuperation which has made us emerge more active than ever from national disasters. Not to go back to the days following the Hundred Years' War[21] or the Revolutionary period, who, in 1871, could fail to admire the determination with which France, dismembered and ruined, set to work and in a few years regained her place among the great nations? And what innumerable proofs we have had of this French energy during the recent war! Think of the conditions under which we took the field. We were not ready. Blinded by our dreams of universal brotherhood, we did not believe that war was possible; and, out of our love of peace, we had forgiven our enemies. Heavy artillery was lacking; our ammunition was scarcely sufficient for one big battle. Trusting in treaties, we had massed our forces on the right while the enemy had treacherously concentrated on our left. And at the first shock our troops were overwhelmed and obliged to fall back as far as Paris. Was that the end of France? Who would not have excused us if, yielding to the inevitable, we had given up the game? But it is precisely when everything seems lost that the old French energy rushes to the rescue. The French rose as one man, in a fury of determination. Joffre held the storm in check, never despaired for a moment, and dreamed of victory in the midst of retreat. Later Foch, imperturbable before the irresistible German onslaught, coolly calculated his plans of attack as he defended the breach, and said, "They shall go no farther!" Our engineers, in no way intimidated by the start which the enemy had got, set to work, swearing that they would outdistance the adversary; and they succeeded. So much for the chiefs, stubborn and immovable in their dogged determination to win. And what shall I say of the masses—of all those millions of men and women who, in their ignorance of our true resources, had only patience for support? Civilians took up ungrateful tasks; they bore without grumbling privation, disappointment, anguish, and sorrow; and not one of them harbored the thought that peace could put an end to their sufferings.

It was at the front, of course, that this virtue of energy shone with the brightest flame: yet where would it have been more excusable to weaken? It is difficult to imagine the trial which our soldiers had to undergo during four long, slow, interminable years. It was not war in the open air—the madness of battle, a sportsmanlike game between two adversaries who look each other straight in the face, and who, honoring one another, can forgive as they fall. It was a perpetual waiting for death—for a lurking and a crafty death that watches for one and comes one knows not whence. It was death without glory, in a trench filled with mud and blood. At its best, it was bare existence in that loathsome mud, in the midst of the sickening odor of corpses whose wild

TEMPERAMENT

eyes haunted the living. The only incidents to break the monotonous watch in the trenches were the shells that exploded without warning and covered the living with the putrescent flesh of the dead, or the passing of a friend blown to pieces in one's arms. And all through this tragedy the rain inexorably fell, more and more thoroughly saturating the earth in which one sank, sending black thoughts into men's minds, evoking the desperate memory of loved ones whom one might never see again.

Such were the moral and physical tortures which the French soldier had to undergo in his interminable defense of the front. And he did not have, like the German, the illusion of victory. He saw part of our country in the enemy's power; he was fighting, it seemed, for a lost cause. It mattered not. He said to himself that he would not yield, and he did not yield. He held doggedly, with desperate endurance. The French endurance! Who, in former times, ever spoke of it? And who will dare, henceforward, to omit it from the list of French qualities?

It existed all the time: it was only awaiting the opportunity to show itself in the light of day. People have talked a good deal about "the French miracle." I do not like the word, because it is false. There was no miracle; there was not even a transformation; there was simply a revelation—striking because produced in tragic circumstances—of a peculiarly French virtue which, in reality, forms the basis of our temperament. It is to this genuine seriousness—an attribute which can, when it is necessary, be transmuted into patience, will power, stoicism—that one must look for the imperishable fabric on which the Frenchman has embroidered the flowers of his gayety, his light-heartedness, and his incorrigible love of life—contradictory qualities, if you insist, but nevertheless able to coexist without mutual detriment. It is their fusion which so often causes the Frenchman to puzzle foreigners by his conduct; and it is their fusion which also lends him the power of being grave without looking sullen, determined without being rigid, and heroic without ceasing to be graceful—which, in a word, permits him, in Montesquieu's phrase, "to do frivolous things seriously and serious things gaily."

III

Intellectual Qualities

AMONG the distinctive traits of the French temperament, I have pointed out the excitability of our nervous system, the impulsiveness of our will. These semi-physiological characteristics have corresponding qualities in the domain of the mind. In individuals gifted with an intense and explosive sensibility, one must expect to find a supple and agile intelligence—an intelligence which goes straight to the facts, grasps them, and immediately translates them into ideas. Facility is, in truth, the foremost intellectual quality of the Frenchman.[1] This natural gift is very striking in our school children, and it has often attracted the attention of foreign educators. I remember conversing with an American professor who had availed himself of a stay in France to investigate our teaching system. He had no words to express his admiration for the precocious alertness and the awakened curiosity of the children whom he had questioned. This quickness of apprehension, when in later years it is supplemented by broader knowledge, is easily transformed into a rather uncommon aptitude for disengaging from the inherently vague and confused complexity of things those essential elements which are the fundamental truths of an otherwise unintelligible whole. The Frenchman instinctively avoids the disorder which overwhelms the mind when it is simultaneously occupied with several ideas. He distinguishes at the first glance, and eliminates, whatever is merely accessory. Following a precept of Voltaire (himself one of the masters of the French method), he perceives that details which lead nowhere are like the impedimenta of an army. He sees "things in a large sense, for the very reason that the human mind is small and that it sinks beneath the weight of detail." Where others would make their way gropingly through the labyrinthine maze of implicit thought, he unhesitatingly puts his finger on the thread which leads him straight to the light of intellectual analysis, and thus enables him to discover the essential. His conviction that no idea is worth anything if it be not the result of exigent selection, has dominated our whole literature from its infancy, and constitutes, in fact, the ruling principle of our habits of thought. To keep one's eyes constantly fixed on the goal; to resist all temptations to stray into bypaths among the undergrowth of ideas, however seductive these may be—that has been the rule observed by all our great writers, novelists, dramatists, critics, and even poets. In this particular our method is the exact opposite of the English method. The Englishman loves to embrace all the details; he often attaches more value to the detail than to the whole. He perceives complexity as clearly as the Frenchman does, or even more clearly; only he does not care to resolve it. He enters into the labyrinth with delight, as a man penetrates into a wild country; he follows all the windings, the least important *détours,* pausing if an object particularly interests him by its novelty or its rarity; nor does he end his minute exploration until he is confident that he has not missed a single point of view that is in any way remarkable. His books are therefore full of observation; they are as rich as life itself; but sometimes—also like life itself—they are somewhat confusing, for the reason that the results of elimination are wanting: the teeming complexity of the world has not been reduced to that simplification which alone can conform the whole to the terms of ordinary human understanding. When the writer is a Shakespeare—when he is one of those colossal geniuses who couple depth and breadth of vision with an instinctive feeling for art—then he obtains results which are unapproachable. But when the artistic sense is only slightly developed, the result is shown in books interesting enough for the richness of their substance, but often formless and capable of giving, at best, no more than an imperfect impression. To a French author these accidents scarcely ever happen. If we cannot pride ourselves on a transcendent genius such as Shakespeare, at least we do not have to suffer that plague known as the amateur. When a French author has any talent whatever, his work may, up to a certain point, be expected to stand the test of time. In any event, his interpretation is always the result of a simplification which disentangles and reveals truth. Whence the seeming paradox that the French, who are accused of being loquacious, express themselves so briefly when they write, whereas the English, unquestionably taciturn, are so prolix in their books.

In submitting himself to this discipline of selection, the Frenchman acquires another intellectual quality: the capacity for generalizing. Simplification and elimination naturally lead him to disengage from each object its essential elements—the residuum which appears as soon as one has isolated the accidental concomitants from the whole. When he has got to this point, it is only a short step for him to discover by comparison the unifying relation among the various particular ideas. To the French mind, generalization is not only a habit: it is a need. And that is why we hold that general ideas are more important than facts. Not that we despise facts, as has sometimes been said: indeed, as we shall see, no people professes a greater respect for realities. But we do not content ourselves with mere statements. We believe that every act, every object, has an implicit meaning which is its unique value, and that that meaning is the essential reality. In other words, facts are to us simply the paving-stones on the road to abstraction. And it is only when we have arrived at the journey's end and embraced the fundamental truths that we feel the sense of having reached our goal.

This tendency does, to be sure, present some dangers. The means whereby one reaches generalization, when used by mediocre minds, sometimes defeat their own object. The aim of the method of selection is to sacrifice the incidental to the principal. But an uncritical mind may be tempted to substitute its own simplicity for the profound truth which it is trying to discover. In undertaking to reduce life to its bare essentials, one risks depriving it of what constitutes its ultimate value and its charm—that is to say, its contrasts, its contradictions; in a word, its mystery. The Frenchman believes that everything is reducible to principles, and that outside the realm of principles no considerable truth can exist. And, in his constant effort to bring order out of chaos, to reduce the incomprehensible to comprehension, he often leads us far from the laughing and populous valleys, to make us climb with him to heights where the atmosphere is doubtless purer and clearer, but also colder. Tasting the joys of abstraction, we lose a little of our humanity.

Still, abstraction and generalization are the best means—the only means—of attaining deep truths. If we simplify the vast mass of human knowledge, we can disentangle the element of identity and universality in things; we can unite a great number of simple ideas in a single vaster and more comprehensive idea. Abstraction and generalization are, therefore, the very conditions without which science could not exist. Without generalization our knowledge would remain mere intuition of isolated single facts and particular objects; and it is precisely because our country has the cult of generalization that she has always been in the first rank of the nations in matters scientific. According to the statement of your compatriot, Mr. Lester Ward, France, "leaving the details and the minutiæ to the German and English schools, forged the chain of science and philosophy."[2] John Theodore Merz admitted the same fact when, in his *History of European Thought,* he said: "In France, during the early part of the century the foundation of nearly all the modern sciences was laid; many of them were brought under the rule of a strict mathematical treatment."[3]

People do not quite do us justice on this point. Our savants do not, to be sure, glory in perfecting the minute applications of a discovery and reducing it to daily use until it has become a household word.

They dedicate themselves rather to the establishment of principles and laws, leaving to others the task of developing all the possibilities inherent in their inventions.[4] But there, precisely, lies the value of their achievements. Their ideas open up new vistas which lead to innumerable practical utilizations; and that is why there are so many Frenchmen among the discoverers of the great fecund ideas. One might, indeed, venture the assertion that every theory which has revolutionized some part of science has been, in its inception, connected with a Frenchman. It is hardly necessary to recall the name of Laplace, who, in his *Exposition du système du monde,* advanced a theory which was the origin of all cosmogonic research; that of Ampère, who, by discovering the action of electric currents on each other, made telegraphy possible; that of Papin, who demonstrated the motive power of steam; that of Sadi Carnot, to whom we must attribute the origin of thermo-dynamics; that of Coulomb, of whom it was said that "entirely by himself he simultaneously founded two sciences which, before his time, were a mere collection of facts and assertions of a purely qualitative character":[5] electro-statics and magnetism; that of Fresnel, an inventive genius of astounding boldness, who demonstrated the vibratory character of light, establishing thus the basic theory of luminous phenomena; that of Lavoisier, who is justly held to be the founder of modern chemistry; that of J. B. Dumas, who, in organic chemistry, was the pioneer of an endless series of discoveries perfected by other Frenchmen, such as Auguste Laurent and Berthelot; that of Haüy, who created, almost alone, the science of crystallography and brought it to such a point that his successors "had scarcely anything left to do but to complete the details of his work";[6] that of Buffon, whose hypotheses dominate geology and modern palæontology; that of Élie de Beaumont, who remains one of the greatest theorists in geology; that of Lamarck, who to-day is admitted to have discovered transformism, thus anticipating Darwin; that of Adolphe Brongniart, who was the real founder of palæobotany; that of Bichat, who, in creating general anatomy, paved the way for histology; that of J. L. A. de Quatrefages, who conceived the idea of studying man according to the methods of natural history, and thus fixed the laws of anthropology, a science for which Broca formulated a method; that of Claude Bernard, who organized experimental physiology and introduced into biology the idea of determinism; and, finally, that of Pasteur, the most prodigious savant of modern times, who, by revealing the rôle played by microbes and by introducing vaccines and serums, accomplished a revolution to which no other is comparable. This single name is alone sufficient to prove the creativeness of French science.[7]

In a word, French science is, in its tendencies as in its methods, eminently philosophical. And that is doubtless why, conversely but logically, our philosophers are so often men of science. On this point M. Bergson once remarked: "French philosophy has always been closely allied to positive science. . . . In Descartes the union between philosophy and mathematics is so close that it is difficult to say whether his geometry was suggested to him by his metaphysic or whether his metaphysic is an extension of his geometry. Pascal was a profound mathematician and a very original physicist before being a philosopher. The philosophy of the eighteenth century found its principal recruits among the geometricians, the naturalists, the doctors (d'Alembert, La Mettrie, Bonnet, Cabanis, and others). In the nineteenth century some of the greatest French thinkers—Auguste Comte, Cournot, Renouvier, and others—arrived at philosophy through the province of mathematics; one of them, Henri Poincaré, was a mathematician of genius. Claude Bernard, who gave us the philosophy of the experimental method, was one of the creators of physiology. And even most of the French philosophers who, during the last century, devoted themselves to introspective study felt the need of searching on the physical side—in physiology, in mental pathology, and elsewhere—for some tangible assurance that they were not giving themselves up to a mere play of ideas, a manipulation of abstract concepts. This tendency is visible as early as the great initiator of the introspective method, Maine de Biran.''[8] M. Bergson, from whom I quote these words, is himself a case in point: for, by his own admission, he has tried "to transport metaphysics into the realm of experience and, by appealing to science and to inner consciousness, and by developing the intuitive faculty, to build up a philosophy capable of furnishing, not only general theories, but also the interpretation of particular concrete facts.''[9]

The fact is that the Frenchman, in his search for the universal, knows how to avoid the pitfalls which menace the too rigorously abstract mind. We may say of those who are obsessed by the passion for general ideas that, "if they abandon themselves too exclusively to such ideas, they tend to pick out more and more from among them the most general—those which apply rather to causes than to effects, rather to essentials than to accidental qualities."[10] They wish to penetrate into the inaccessible depths of the absolute, and they end by losing all contact with reality. Whence, for example, the German's love of metaphysics. The Frenchman, on the contrary, instinctively abhors all that is indefinite and incapable of analysis. It is not that he shrinks from bold hypotheses—as is shown by the work of Descartes, in which M. Bergson finds the germ of nearly all the celebrated systems of modern times, and by the lofty speculations of a Malebranche or a Maine de Biran. But he wisely renounces subjects in which the mind has not the clear light of reflection to guide it. He cannot bear to let his mind wander in the misty fields of the unknowable. It is impossible for him to found systems on the shifting sand of conjecture. He always feels the need of keeping to the real. And as soon as, by an effort of analysis, he has embraced a general truth, he knows how to stop at the precise point beyond which, if he were to plunge forward too far into abstraction, he risks losing sight of the original facts. Having thoroughly mastered and consolidated his position, he retraces his steps, armed by the principles which he has discovered, and again searches for the original facts—not, indeed, to the end of building up grandiose interpretations of the universe, but in order to test the consequences of his general truth.

In this new effort of his thought the Frenchman

is helped by his taste for deductive reasoning. For his essentially abstract and analytical mind is also accustomed by training to synthetic methods. This is, without doubt, a result of our Latin education, and perhaps also of the influence which scholasticism exercised on our way of thinking during the Middle Ages and even long after. For scholasticism is a method which became peculiarly French. "In the University of Paris," as has been said, "scholasticism was born, grew, and died." It was still followed in France at a time when Germany was already intoxicated by mysticism. In any case the syllogistic method has always remained our favorite.[11] The Frenchman has, unquestionably, a taste for demonstration. He sees everything under the aspect of a combination of proofs and necessary consequences. Since he excels in discovering the logical chain of things and in determining their relation to one another, he is always ready to establish the truth or falsehood of a proposition by rigorous reasoning; and he has an incontestable talent for presenting the facts in a luminous order which makes the relations of cause to effect and of truth to truth stand out clearly—a talent for uniting them with such perfect coherence that his order becomes in itself almost a proof. This it was that made John Stuart Mill say of the sociologist Auguste Comte that he gave to his ideas such a systematic and compact form that they had almost the appearance of science itself.

We have, indeed, such a belief in the value of logic and so much confidence in its power that when we have come to a clear conclusion, this conclusion easily takes in our eyes the form of absolute and irrefutable truth. It is, with us, an axiom that "Truth is one." Whereas an Englishman will admit in his confident opportunism that there may be in every situation two truths, one absolute and theoretic, the other relative and contingent, the Frenchman obstinately maintains that facts are facts, that they have a precise meaning, and that between two divergent opinions one must make a choice. In reply to the arguments which give too large a place to the mere accident of circumstance, he opposes this final statement, which, to him, is not even open to discussion: "Truth is truth."

But, if truth is one, all that is divergent from it is error. And as we love truth with a passionate fervor, we take no ease until we have destroyed the error. It seems to us that no one can enjoy his convictions in peace so long as he remains threatened by a negation. Thence comes that earnestness which urges us to pursue in our neighbors all opposition to our own beliefs as if it were an insult to eternal truth. We rise up, combative, aggressive, the ardent champions of this truth. We who, in ordinary life, can give proof of such breadth of mind become uncompromising when it is a question of ideas. Men and things matter little, provided that principles are safe! For this reason, no country exists in which quarrels over opinions are more numerous or more fierce. Be it a question of whether the ancients or the moderns are the more original, or whether Joan of Arc was a saint or just a poor girl; be it a question of defending or attacking a religious dogma, or of re-trying a case in the law courts—to everything, from philosophy to politics, we bring the same rigorousness, the same inflexibility. Directly a debate is raised to the heights of thought, it is immediately pursued with a sort of fanatical ardor.

This violence in our discussions is so extreme that it has sometimes helped to spread strange opinions about us. It has been concluded that Frenchmen must indeed be divided, for a state of such intractable hatred to exist among them. In truth, all these disagreements and disputes are only the rather ardent manifestations of one fundamental virtue of the French mind, in which all such disagreements can be reconciled—intellectual probity. We respect truth so much that we are ready to sacrifice to it friendship, comfort, and even our most vital interests. "It is a greater perfection to recognize truth, even if it be to our disadvantage, than to be blind to it," said Descartes. All Frenchmen agree on this point, even if they are in adverse camps. And this is the saving grace of our *intransigeance,* the thing that makes it worthy of respect. For if, in defending our beliefs too ardently, we imperil our intellectual agility, we at any rate owe to this ardor a quality without which no sound or correct thinking were possible—sincerity.

This sincerity, moreover, is allied quite naturally to that other belief which makes us submit to the laws of reason, in which we see the mind's most perfect instrument. If we attach so much value to true ideas, it is because we are convinced of the infallibility of this function—the very source of all thought—which enables us to interpret experience impersonally, according to the universal principles of things. We willingly repeat with La Bruyère: "Reason is of the essence of truth; it is one"; and this suffices to confirm us in the conviction that error cannot triumph when the clear light of understanding is cast upon it.

This is a very old belief with us. Perhaps we must look for its origin—as for that of our taste for deductive reasoning—in the influence exercised on our ancestors by the Latin culture; for the Romans, following the Greek example, had also entrusted to Reason the task of directing their actions. And, here too, scholasticism played its part. In the midst of contentions that were often sterile, this philosophical school unceasingly tried to submit faith to the scrutiny of intelligence. In a peculiarly French form it ended in an attempt to reconcile Faith and Reason. Abelard professed that in its own domain Reason was the sole mistress. He upheld the statement that the dogma is incontestable, but that it can be demonstrated. And his method actually "prevailed in the University of Paris of the twelfth and thirteenth centuries."[12]

And Descartes, "in constituting Reason sole judge of truth,"[13] merely gave the support of a coherent system to what was already a secular and national certainty. We know how the seventeenth century adopted Cartesianism and conformed to rules which so well suited its own tendencies. The *Discours de la Méthode* not only marked the starting point of a philosophy: it was also the breviary of men of fashion when they wanted to satisfy their intellectual aspirations. And thus it definitely established the dogma of Reason and crystallized forever in France the taste for abstract ideas. In the seventeenth century, at all events, we find the very mainspring of the works of our national authors, whether orators, dramatists, or poets, in a philosophical notion issuing from the profoundest part of our intelligence. Molière and Bossuet are inspired by Reason; and so are Boileau and Corneille. Did not even Pascal, who so powerfully invoked the intangible character of Faith, see in Reason a means of bringing back the skeptical to a belief in Religion?[14] The eighteenth century went still farther in this direction. The period of Descartes had taught that there was a domain into which Reason could penetrate only with infinite precaution and great humility. Descartes warned the mind against the narrowness of a method which presumed to submit to the understanding even that which the understanding could not grasp. But in the eighteenth century Reason boldly asserted its supremacy and claimed predominance. It did violence to Faith and reduced her to silence. This triumph was such that Reason abandoned the province of reality and "worked only on ideas."[15] The thinkers of the time were all more or less like the poet La Motte, of whom Fontenelle said that he "raised in his mind a temple to his own Reason."[16]

To-day this long education has produced all its logical effects, and they are probably irrevocable. If the end of the eighteenth century and the beginning of the nineteenth, in their reaction against the excessive rationalism of the preceding age, restored sentiment to its legitimate place, it is none the less true that the French intelligence is still based on "the belief that in the reality of things all is intelligible—if not by the light of our science as it is now, still imperfect, at any rate by the light of science in its ultimate perfection."[17] And Reason is still the guide whom, by preference, we choose.

Our confidence in Reason is so unshakable that this faculty is no longer the privilege of an intellectual élite. It is to be found to-day in all ranks of society. In its popular form it has become that common sense which is certainly one of the characteristic qualities of our nation. Common sense is, after all, only the faculty of appreciating practical things in a sane way; it is critical Reason taken in its most concrete form and applied to the affairs of every-day life. This "power of judging well," as Descartes said, is perhaps the gift that is most nearly common to all Frenchmen. It is equally innate, though in different degrees, in the middle, laboring, and peasant classes. It was this power which made a statesman say that to govern France one needed more common sense than genius.

Our common sense is especially shown in an invisible mistrust of everything exaggerated, exorbitant, or excessive; for whatever is abnormal does not subscribe to the laws of Reason. We love moderation and equilibrium, a good medium course. We agree with Philinte that

> La parfaite raison fuit toute extrêmité
> Et veut que l'on soit sage avec sobriété.

> The ripened judgment shuns all wild extravagance,
> Nor wisdom's self ensues beyond the pale of sense.

Eccentricity shocks us, and we have done away with it. In our country you do not see those fantastic individuals who, in other countries, roam about loose and inflict their oddities on their neighbors. The man who, under a cloak of eccentricity, tries to impose upon us, wastes his time and trouble. Strange sects with burlesque rites have succeeded no better than have the efforts of vulgar advertising. And our common sense is not only an obstacle to foolishness or charlatanism: it is also a moderating influence upon our intellectual life. Our craving for logic, when it becomes excessive, might carry us away and lead us into impossible positions, as indeed it has sometimes done. This is all the more likely because our tendency is toward theories and systems. But directly this danger appears, our good sense intervenes. It dissipates the misty visions of a self-intoxicated intellectualism and brings us quickly back to reality. So it is that, by a curious twist, this French common sense, offspring of Reason and, through it, of all that is most abstract in the mind, turns into an instrument of the practical instinct, and becomes finally the most powerful antidote against the intoxication of Reason itself.

And now, if you combine under the ægis of Reason the qualities which we have recognized as being characteristic of the French mind, you will obtain another of those intellectual qualities: lucidity. For it happens that the operations which regulate our whole manner of thinking are precisely those which almost inevitably produce that clearness in the presentation of ideas and that clarity of expression which have always marked French writers.

It is first of all by generalization that one obtains the unity of a subject. Now, unity is the first condition and, as it were, the focal point of lucidity. It

INTELLECTUAL QUALITIES

might be compared to one of those well-drawn perspectives which enable you to embrace at a glance the long road which you are about to travel. By furnishing the essential and comprehensive idea to which all the secondary ideas lead, it opens the central avenue on which the other roads of thought debouch, and whence it is possible to project light on the remotest quarters of a subject.

It is by the application of logical methods that one groups ideas within this unity, according to an arrangement that can be readily grasped. One might say that the whole art of composition lies in the rigorous coördination of the development. "Style," said Buffon, "is only the order and the movement which we give to our thoughts. If we link them closely together, if we constrict them, the style becomes firm, nervous, and concise; if we allow them to follow one another slowly, only joined together by aimless words, however beautiful the latter may be, the style will be diffuse, weak, and dragging." To put each part in its proper place, to deduce the secondary thoughts rigorously from the principal ones, to unite them one to another according to the connections of dependence which logically govern them and in such a way that they form a chain from which no argument could be omitted without weakening or obscuring the rest; to observe all the way the natural hierarchy of ideas, to pass from the simple to the complex, so that the interest shall not be merely sustained, but shall continuously increase until the conclusion or ultimate unfolding of the essential and profound truth which has been pursued throughout the development, and of which each part was only a contributory fragment—such are the rules by virtue of which our writers obtain those harmonious and convincing wholes which lead the reader by easy paths through the mazes of thought, give him the pleasure of foreseeing the end, make him unconsciously use his reason, and so obtain a solidity, a strength, which disorganized argument, even though it be inspired by genius, can never give.

Finally, it is the process of selection which, in the polishing of style, leads to that absolute inevitability of phrase and that conciseness which give to thought a form under which the idea appears as through a crystal. This pruning has always been the chief preoccupation of French writers. It led to perfection a Pascal, a Bossuet, as well as a Flaubert and a Chateaubriand. Pascal wrote the eighteenth of his *Lettres Provinciales* thirteen times, and he apologized for not having made the sixteenth shorter—a clear proof that he felt compression to be a sure criterion of excellence. La Rochefoucauld offers an even more striking example. No writer, perhaps, ever attained a more dazzling lucidity; and this lucidity, as the study of his manuscripts shows us, was almost entirely obtained by an ever-increasing conciseness. He was never satisfied. When he had found the exact word, he wanted still more brevity. To correct, to him, meant almost invariably to lighten and concentrate the sentence. He suppressed the tiniest superfluities, condensing whole phrases into one word, never tiring of this work of retrenchment, and stopping only when the thought, stripped of all useless clothing, appeared to him in its splendid nudity.[18]

Such is the secret of French lucidity; and one can

see, from its very nature, how complex it is. For it is an error to think that our lucidity is allied to simplicity—or, as our detractors go so far as to say, to superficiality. They contrast it with the German obscurity of style, with the implication that the German obscurity corresponds to an innate profundity of which that obscurity is the evident sign. It is true that our writers, even when they are dealing with philosophical subjects, do not bristle with formidable, abstract, and pedantic terms—a convenient way of hiding the triteness, the poverty, and the incompleteness of an idea. They address themselves, not merely to a small group of initiates, but to all those who are capable of judging. They use everyday language, convinced that there is no concept, however new or subtle, for which the common linguistic heritage cannot suffice. That is why they express themselves so simply that the philosopher and the savant are no more difficult to understand than any other writer. And that is precisely what makes people doubt the value of their works. Is it possible to be both profound and intelligible? they wonder. Those who reason thus forget that for obscurity there may be many reasons, of which the principal is the impotence of the mind to find its way through the confusion of instinctive mental processes. But French lucidity, when it is of good quality, is the proof that understanding has penetrated so deeply into the chaos of things as to reach that hidden point at which the truth, the explanation and solution of this chaos, hunted down to its last entrenchments, yields itself to us free from the mists that usually becloud it. For "it is not on the surface, it is at the greatest depths, that the simple truth lies; and there, too, lucidity is found."[19] If you desire a proof of what I state, I advise you to read —it is one example among many—the *Introduction à l'Etude de la Médecine Expérimentale,* by Claude Bernard. You will see how, in this unequalled work, lucidity, depth, and truth become interchangeable terms.

The value of the French lucidity was recognized by the younger Fichte at a time when the Germans had not yet acquired the habit of disparaging the rest of the universe. "What distinguishes the French in their scientific productions," he said, "and what has a deeper connection than people suppose with the real appreciation of truth, is the lucidity, the harmonious completeness of the idea, the rigorousness with which it is stated, and the clarity of the definitions. As a rule they (the French) are less apt than we to reach extreme conclusions. . . . It must be admitted that the French possess precisely those qualities which we lack—qualities the acquisition of which becomes more and more imperative. At the same time we must take care not to yield the superiority of thought and of scientific depth to this neighboring people who are developing with such rapidity and energy. It is in this, so far as German philosophy is concerned, that the importance of the French mind and the influence which it should exercise on us consist. By the degree in which the French assimilate our theories, we can recognize the degree of finality of those theories. They are the first and the most unanswerable judges of the lucidity, maturity, and truth of an idea."[20] And, in admitting this, Fichte at the same time defined the true scope of this gift. The French lucidity

INTELLECTUAL QUALITIES

is, in truth, less a special characteristic than a combination. It is the resultant of all the qualities, native or acquired, which go to the making up of a French brain, and which by happy chance not only combine, but complete each other, thus mutually acquiring complementary force before melting into the sovereign faculty which includes them all—Reason. It is the concrete expression of all that is most essential in our mind, the visible sign of our supreme intellectuality.

And with these words we may end this chapter, for they sum up exactly what has just been said. It has often been remarked that we are the most purely intellectual people of the modern world. Even in the Middle Ages one of the most frequently repeated sayings was that "Empire belonged to Germany, religious dominion to Italy, and scientific preëminence to France."[21] The centuries have only added to the truth of the remark. Is it because our literature goes back into the most remote antiquity that our intellects to-day are of such keenness for the operations of thoughts? I do not know. But it is certain that no people has in like degree the cult of the Idea—one might actually say, worship of the Idea. We think for the pleasure of thinking, and to the free play of our intellectual activity we are ready to sacrifice everything. There is perhaps no quality more typical of us than this, and it has influenced our entire way of feeling and of living. We shall find innumerable proofs of this no later than in the next chapter, in which we shall see how the refinement of our intelligence has modified the fundamental character of the French imagination.

IV

Imagination

THE intellectual qualities of the typical Frenchman are quite determinate, and no one gainsays them. But their very existence is often invoked as a proof that we are deficient in other qualities. Some critics, laying stress on a supposed incompatibility between imagination and the power of abstraction, affirm that the French cannot enjoy the intoxicating visions of fancy. Mr. Brownell, for instance, asserts that our superlative aptitude for Reason and sociability is gained only at the cost of our poetical sense.[1] And Mr. Brander Matthews proposed the same idea in other words when he noted the absence in our nature of "that energy that is peculiar to the Anglo-Saxon race and which is often translated into imagination."[2]

Such statements are strange enough. They do not agree with that other belief according to which intellectual vivacity is one of the principal characteristics of our temperament. For is not the rapid conception of ideas the essential condition and, as it were, the first degree of all creative fancy? My experience—and it is not exceptional—shows me that there is no one more fundamentally imaginative than the Frenchman. Consider, for example, the pleasure he takes in playing that game of illusions known as building castles in Spain. That lesser form of imagination which consists in sketching a whole novel out of a trivial incident—a meeting, the receipt of a letter, a word overheard by chance—is one in which our fancy most readily indulges itself in idle moments. M. Ribot gives a typical example of it in his book called *Imagination Créatrice*.[3] One of his correspondents confesses to him that "if, at church or at the theatre, in a public square or in a railway station, his attention is attracted by a person, man or woman, he at once reconstructs that person's present, his past, his kind of life, his occupations, from his appearance, dress, and gait; he imagines the quarter of the town which he inhabits, his lodging, his furniture, and so on." In France the people are legion who similarly create an artificial world in which, by figments of the imagination, they relieve the monotony of humdrum life and pursue the accomplishment of their desires in the imaginary world of daydreams. I could give you innumerable examples by merely looking around me in the circle of my own friends and relatives. And there is no doubt that this is a habit which has sprung from the very depths of our being. As early as the seventeenth century it was caught and perpetuated in a never-fading picture by our great fabulist, who was also a great psychologist. In his fable of "The milkmaid and the pitcher of milk," La Fontaine,[4] when he showed us Perrette building up all her fortune on the hope of a problematical gain, was merely representing that same inveterate characteristic of the French disposition, which is always being prompted by its innate optimism to pursue chimeras:—

Quel esprit ne bat la campagne?
Qui ne fait châteaux en Espagne?
Quand je suis seul, je fais au plus brave un défi;
Je m'écarte, je vais détrôner le sophi;
   On m'élit roi, mon peuple m'aime;
Les diadèmes vont sur ma tête pleuvant.

What man dupes not himself amain?
Who builds no castle towers in Spain?
The boldest I defy—when I'm alone;
Go to, I'll pull the sufi from his throne!
   A doting people crowns me king,
And diadems come raining on my brow.

A glance at the development of our literature shows at once that we have had our fair share of imaginative writers. What country ever produced a period more completely given over to dreams than our Middle Ages? For several centuries poetry was the form to which French thought naturally resorted; and we may say that during that whole era our ancestors lived in a world peopled by magnificent and mysterious visions, and that with these visions they satisfied the desires for the unknown which filled their ardent and simple minds. The way of escape into a beatific land they found first of all through our rich religious literature, with the inexhaustible marvels of its biblical stories, its lives of the Virgin and the saints. And, beside these semi-mystical works, what a prodigious flowering of romanesque literature! a heterogeneous mixture of *chansons de geste,* tales about the crusades, and ancient fables of Celtic heroes, in which were conjured up fabulous countries and supernatural beings—invincible knights, magicians and enchanters, terrible giants and malicious dwarfs, all engaged in miraculous adventures; the whole forming a cycle of fables of such unbridled fantasy as sometimes to degenerate into extravagance.

And, ever since that remote time when our national genius revealed itself thus in one of its essential aspirations, the same longing to create a supernatural world in which the mind can be free from reality has never ceased to be made manifest among us. What obscures the fact is that, from the Renaissance, all the forces of the intellect, led by Reason, leagued themselves against pure imagination. But their triumph was more apparent than real. Even if the imaginative faculty was forced at times to submit, it did not go out of existence or relax its hold upon our inward life. In the sixteenth century imagination remained the motive force behind the healthy realism and overflowing gayety of a Rabelais, the debonair philosophical vagaries of a Montaigne. In the seventeenth century the passion for the romanesque continued to triumph, in the face of the Cartesian tyranny and despite the authority of Reason. Incredible stories were set in pastoral surroundings and imaginary landscapes. The taste for adventure more than ever demanded an outlet, and found it in works—epic poems or romances—in which fantastically brave and noble heroes perform stupendous feats of swordsmanship. In the middle of the century the passion for this sort of romance was such that, if we are to believe Charles Sorel, ''more than one young man almost lost his reason by this kind of reading.''[5] Even those authors who followed another bent, and sought to introduce a little reality into their works by depicting fashionable sentiments or by representing contemporary types under figurative names—Mademoiselle de Scudéry, for example—could not help piling up adventures and sprinkling their stories with impossibilities.

And this century, supposedly so rational, gave enthusiastic welcome to a literature of the marvellous which harks back to certain creations of the Middle Ages. The *Contes de Perrault* opened a door for the return of some of the characters already encountered in our old romances, easily recognizable under thin disguises—fairies good or bad, ogres, talking animals. And immediately there was a veritable explosion of fairy lore. Everybody began to write "Mother Goose tales." The Comtesse d'Aulnoy published her *Contes Nouveaux ou les Fées à la Mode;* M. de Lesconvel entered the lists with his *Illustres Fées,* and the Sieur de Preschac with his *Contes Moins Contes, Sans Parangon et la Reine des Fées.* The Comtesse d'Auneuil followed with *La Tyrannie des Fées Détruites.* Fénelon himself did not disdain to put his most melodious pen to the service of old nurse's tales. So abundant was this imaginative production that in 1785 it was possible to gather under the title *Cabinet des Fées* no fewer than forty volumes containing only the best examples of these tales of wonder.[6]

It would seem at first glance that during the eighteenth century imagination was indeed driven out of French literature. But the domination of the philosophers was in vain. Though formally banished, Imagination only burned more ardently in men's minds. We must remember that this century showed an instinctive love for Shakespeare and

IMAGINATION

greeted Rousseau with enthusiasm; that the Arabian Nights' were its delight; and that it gathered together, as we have just seen, the stories of the preceding age. People discussed philosophy—but for their recreation they devoured the *Cabinet des Fées.* Voltaire himself wrote *Micromégas,* a fantasy in the manner of Swift; Montesquieu, the author of *L'Esprit des Lois,* is also the author of the *Temple de Gnide;* Diderot, the founder of the *Encyclopédie,* charmed the salons of the time with *L'Oiseau Blanc* and *Les Bijoux Indiscrets;* Bernardin de Saint-Pierre, out of the mists of his utopian dreams, discovered exoticism; and Cazotte audaciously asserted his right to the marvelous with his *Diable Amoureux,* which a few years later was to inspire Hoffman.

These fits of independence prove that during all this time the forces of imagination were accumulating and becoming, perhaps, all the stronger for having been sternly repressed. Thus, when Romanticism broke out, it did not discover imagination under the influence of foreign works, as is constantly asserted: it merely released what was already there. Sentiment, too long repressed, burst its barriers. The writers of the period admitted this general truth by tracing their own lineage back to the Middle Ages. And, in this modern fulfilment, French imagination, if less naïve than in the early days of our literature, lost nothing of its vigor, its buoyancy. The Romantic Period is second to none in the richness of its poetic visions. The bare phrase is enough to evoke the magnificent pageant of those writers who gave luster to this period of our literary history—Chateaubriand, the most essentially imaginative being who ever existed, the incarnate spirit of dream, a restless soul athirst for beauty, tireless in his efforts to flee from reality and to find in the enchantment of changing sensations or in the splendor of visions an antidote to his incurable weariness of life; Lamartine, the most spontaneous of the lyric poets, of whom it has been truly said that he was poetry personified, for he poured forth his melancholy and tender soul, his boundless yearning, in strains of such enchanting harmony that they seem less a literary expression than the natural outburst of his sensitive nature; Musset, the Ariel of our literature, a unique blend of quivering passion and fantasy, who so incomparably evokes all the fancies that can glint and glimmer in a mind as sprightly, graceful, and lightsome as a sylph; George Sand, who so adored the romantic that she wove it into her own life, tirelessly pursuing an impossible ideal—now sentimental, now lyric, now humanitarian, but always chimerical—through the multitudinous adventures of the unbridled imagination which was the essence of her genius; and finally Victor Hugo, who alone would suffice to undermine the legend of the Frenchman alien to the poetic—Victor Hugo, the Michael Angelo of language, the inspired welder of gorgeous metaphor, the great magician evoking with his wand the most dazzling pictures, myths, symbols, fantastic visions—always tumultuous, torrential, and overwhelming, even when he tries to be tender. Is it an exaggeration to say that rarely has any country shown in one generation a richer or more varied galaxy of imaginative writers?

With the school that followed Romanticism, the French imagination had once again to withstand the onslaught of Reason. For lyric abandon, realism would substitute an art with no other aim than to reproduce life exactly. The realists affected impassibility; they gave observation the place of honor; they actually aimed at the coldness of science. But even here imagination held its own. It had its revenge on those very writers who pretended to banish it; it cried aloud in their works and gave the lie to their theories. Save for a few rare exceptions, our most convinced realists tacitly accepted the favors of imagination, even when they believed themselves freed from its dominion. Flaubert is only a romantic who missed his vocation, and whose bitter destiny it was to be compelled to stifle his longings for the mysterious, the exotic, and the strange (witness his youthful works and the *Tentation de Saint-Antoine*) and to force himself to that labor of patient observation which he laid upon himself. Daudet likewise based his novels—ostensibly—on a rigorous documentation; yet what is he if not a lyric writer who, even in the most impersonal of his works, somehow contrives to let us hear the secret vibration of a soul quivering with poetry? And it is the same with Zola, the head of our naturalistic school. He posed as the physiologist of fiction. But in spite of his desire to compose purely scientific works he remained the most undisciplined of imaginative writers. His novels are true poems which often attain to an epic grandeur. He is the Victor Hugo of naturalism. His descriptions, as M. Lanson said,[3] "are intense, brilliant, overwhelming; they are almost hallucinations; M. Zola's eye, or rather his pen, deforms and exaggerates all objects. What he shows us is a monstrous dream of life, not a bare transcription of reality. His unbridled imagination animates all lifeless forms; Paris, a mine, a department store, a locomotive become terrifying beings instinct with desires, menacing, devouring, suffering; the kaleidoscope dances before our eyes as in a nightmare.''

There is actually in Zola a sort of vision which makes him prototypical of the fantastic writers. And never has this kind of writing been more in vogue than in our own day. Romanticism, with Charles Nodier, Gérard de Nerval, and Théophile Gautier, had already appealed to superstition and evoked supernatural beings—fairies, goblins, ghosts—and created strange and mysterious personages. But it would seem as if the last half century has actually seen a strengthening of this inveterate impulse of ours to remould the world in such wise as to free it from the natural laws of life. We have experienced a succession of works the authors of which exploit emotions of fear and wonder common to all men, describe strange pathological states, and conjure up impressions of a world of unknown forces, the influence of which, though experienced, remains inexplicable, and which strikes uneasiness or terror to the soul. It would take too long to cite the array of authors who have extended the domain of French imagination to these ultimate bounds. I will only remind you of a few of the best known: Barbey d'Aurevilly, Balzac (in his philosophical works such as *Louis Lambert, Séraphita, La Peau de Chagrin*), Paul Feval, Mérimée, Maupassant (the Maupassant of *Sur l'Eau, La Peur, Le Horla*), Villiers de l'Isle Adam, Léon Hennique, Jules Verne, J. H. Rosny the elder, Maurice Renard, J. Hoche, Henri de

Régnier, Pierre Véber, Claude Farrère.[9] The success of M. Pierre Benoist's *Atlantide* is an excellent proof of the influence which this kind of literature still exerts on the French mind—a mind persistently romantic, even when it imagines itself to be most practical.

Nor is this all. So far, I have considered only that kind of imagination which wrests beauty or mystery from the world in order to form new visions by unexpected combinations—that "misleading faculty," as Pascal would have said, which creates illusions. It is the type of imagination which is most widely known; the only one which matters to the crowd, and perhaps to many critics as well. For, in the popular belief, there is no imagination without a certain wildness, as is shown in the portrait which Shakespeare drew of the poet, brother to the madman and the lover, whose eye,

> . . . in a fine frenzy rolling,
> Doth glance from heaven to earth, from earth to heaven,
> And, as imagination bodies forth
> The form of things unknown, the poet's pen
> Turns them to shapes and gives to airy nothings
> A local habitation and a name.

But, side by side with the writers who have in them this power of roaming the universe on the wings of exaltation in such a way as to assemble forms, sounds, and colors into a new world of splendid or fantastic visions, a dazzling web embroidered with a thousand fragments of transfigured truth—side by side with these, there is room for other dreamers who know how to evoke ideas more intimate, one might almost say more spiritual. For it is not only by the use of the concrete elements furnished by the visible universe that images are created. Visions may well up from the depths of our minds by the more secret process of drawing on the mass of emotions and ideas accumulated within us. M. Paul Bourget defined this distinction with his habitual acumen when he said:[10] "In considering the human brain as a reproductive machine, Flaubert justly observed that this cerebral reproduction does not apply merely to the scenes of the external world as our different senses represent them. There is a teeming inner world—ideas, volitions, which suggest to us images of an order quite distinct from the other. If we shut our eyes and think of some past event— a farewell, for instance—purely physical details will be recalled to memory: a landscape, the tone of a voice, a look, a gesture; and at the same time there will arise the feelings which we experienced in that landscape, when we heard that voice, when we saw that look." In other words, there are two very different sorts of imagination. While the first—the one with which I have dealt thus far—borrows its materials from the spectacle of the external world, the second, which we may call internal, deals with the ideas, feelings, and emotions suggested by that same spectacle. It is, so to speak, imagination in the next higher degree, for it goes farther than sensation pure and simple, with which the other is content, and tries to extricate the intellectual or emotional meaning hidden at the core of sensation. It results from an alliance of the "subjectivity of pure imagination with the objectivity of rational processes."[11] Its distinguishing mark is that it is an imagination the functioning of which is always under the control of the intellect.

Now the Frenchman, precisely because he worships intelligence, feels himself to be peculiarly sympathetic to this kind of imagination; and the more he comes under the sway of reason, the more surely this kind of imagination develops in him. Seemingly a paradox, this law has only to be reflected upon to appear as a truism. For whenever reason exerts its power over the mind unstably or incompletely, outraged imagination only reacts the more strongly, and always ends by triumphing, as it did over Zola; whereas when reason is fully ascendant, since it cannot possibly smother the instinctive need of imagination it is forced to find a *modus vivendi* between itself and that need. An equilibrium is established between the opposing forces; and this equilibrium favors that combination of pure imagination with intelligence, each interpenetrating and also limiting the other, which is, as we have seen, the formula of internal imagination.

It is now clear why this internal imagination is so widespread in France. It is not always recognized, for on account of its hybrid composition it varies enormously and may assume all sorts of individual disguises. But it has affected every literary type, even those which are deemed refractory to all imagination; and to try to follow it through its multitudinous transformations would almost necessitate writing the entire history of French thought. I shall content myself, therefore, with studying it in the three forms which it has most often assumed in France: the scientific, the historic, and the psychological.

The two words "scientific" and "imagination," thus brought together, seem ill-assorted; but their association expresses a great truth. The prejudgment that science and imagination are antagonistic rests on a false interpretation of the two terms. Imagination is as necessary to the savant as is the reasoning faculty, for without it he would remain locked in a vicious circle of propositions and categories, without direction or outcome. Pasteur (a capital example of the inventive genius), although he was the most scrupulous of observers, recognized that "the illusions of the experimenter are a part of his strength; it is his preconceived ideas which serve him for guide."[12] To discover the truth, indeed, one must first conceive it as a hypothesis. Now, what is a hypothesis if not a gathering together of ideas until then isolated, but capable of being united by association? that is to say, What is it but an image created by the same means which are used to produce poetic figures? Only the *matter* of the image differs, it being fashioned in this case out of concepts and not out of forms or concrete objects. The mental process is the same.

What I have already said of French science will now enable you to understand without further explanation why scientific imagination is peculiarly characteristic of the French mind. If our savants are outstanding in their aptitude for invention, it is precisely because they are gifted with that kind of internal imagination which formulates those abstractions known as preconceived ideas, by the aid of which men build up the new and unexplored world which, when verified and realized by experience, becomes to-morrow's familiar truth.

IMAGINATION

Buffon is a very good example of our scientific imagination. He was, whatever may be said, a great savant; he had the essential qualities, the twin gifts of observation and deduction. But when the data were insufficient, he had recourse to the most powerful imagination ever granted to man to help him fathom the mystery of matter. As soon as Buffon had gathered a certain number of isolated facts, he could rise by an effort of intuition to the most amazing generalizations. In the simple drawing together of statements without apparent connection he at once saw resemblances and links which could be translated into conjectures; whence some of the most brilliant contributions ever made to our knowledge of the universe. It was thus that, like a true seer, in moments of exaltation comparable to poetic enthusiasm, he first envisaged scientific theories which have been epoch-making. He had a forethought of the mutability of species; he foresaw transformism; he nearly sketched the theory of evolution. By imagination alone he discovered in one flash what others were not able to establish save after endless observations.

The scientific imagination, made manifest in this degree, is no whit inferior to the boldest lyric imagination. The historic imagination, of which I am now going to speak, does not require so strenuous an effort. But it, too, presupposes the creation of a world which does not fall under direct observation. One may define it as the power of bringing back to life by means of documentary evidence the peoples and the life of an older time. The real historian, indeed, is he who, through "authentic texts and the deeds and actions of which these texts give him a glimpse, can penetrate, by means of an intuitive effort similar to that of the poet or novelist, the inner being of historic personages; can see them act and move, can think with them and conjecture the motives which directed their actions.'"[13] It is solely on these conditions that he is able to create a work not only interesting, but true. For the school which pretends to see in history only the bare, dry enumeration of facts which must be treated with the coldest impassibility, lest the introduction of one's personality be a cause of error, creates mere industrious mechanics, but not true historians. History cannot be dissociated from life. It is a past life, a petrified life; but it is life nevertheless, and to refuse to reanimate it is to betray it by robbing it of its essential manifestation and of its very reason for existence. In order to reconstruct the past, the historian needs imagination just as much as the man of science does when he enlarges the domain of the future.

We find an arresting description of the *modus operandi* of the historical imagination, as here conceived, in the account which Augustin Thierry gave of his own experiences. He related[14] how, winter and summer, he would haunt the libraries in his search for materials for the works on which he was engaged. His enthusiasm was so great that he had come to live as in a dream. Entirely engrossed in his labors, he was oblivious of what happened around him. Readers would come to the tables and go from them; the library assistants and the general public would cross and recross the room; he noticed nothing. He saw only the vision called up by what he read. By allowing his mind to wander at will among the documents he acquired a unique faculty which enabled him "to read by intuition, as it were, and almost immediately to find the passage" that interested him. "His vital force seemed to be entirely directed toward one single point." And in the sort of ecstasy that inwardly absorbed him, while his hand turned the leaves or took notes, the bygone ages appeared to him with the vividness of reality. He felt himself transported among the men of primitive times, he watched their strange deeds and unfamiliar customs, he shared their joys and sorrows—in a word, he lived their life. And from this vision there emerged those vividly picturesque masterpieces, *La Conquête de l'Angleterre par les Normands* and *Récits Mérovingiens*. These works may since have been surpassed in exactitude, but they have never been equaled in dramatic force and movement; indeed, they have an incomparable human value.

The type of imagination which characterizes the works of Augustin Thierry is found in all our historians—in all those, at least, who have not been led astray by certain very different methods imported from across the Rhine. It varies in intensity, of course, according to the individual temperament. In Michelet, for example, it becomes so vehement as to be almost abnormal. The author of *L'Histoire de France* believed with Augustin Thierry that history should be a "resurrection." His erudition was wide and varied, for, more than any of his predecessors, he had delved among the treasures of our national archives and minutely studied all that would help him to bring our country's past back to life—manuscripts, monuments, inscriptions, coins. What seized upon the arid documents, however, was the most intensely lyrical temperament conceivable; and from the union in him of learning and poetry there was born a historical vision so glowing that few are comparable to it outside the burning pictures drawn by that other visionary, Thomas Carlyle. So great was Michelet's power of evocation that in the best passages of his work—those in which truth is not distorted by the passion of the doctrinaire—his imagination became a veritable instrument of scientific research.

It is evident that historical imagination of this order cannot be common. As a general rule the historical imagination is more restrained; and by being restrained it may the better approximate that delicate equilibrium of inspiration and intelligence which is its distinctive mark. It is then to be recognized by such a mixture of erudition and power to re-create the life of past centuries as gives free play to both the critical faculties and the ability to imagine glowing pictures. Such, at least, are the qualities which distinguish the best of our modern historians—Georges Perrot, Gaston Boissier, Albert Sorel, Ernest Lavisse, Camille Jullian, Gabriel Hanotaux, J. J. Jusserand, Imbart de Latour, Albert Vandal, and especially the master of them all, Fustel de Coulanges, who united in himself the most invaluable qualities of savant, writer, and artist—learning, scientific exactitude, philosophical breadth of generalization, and lucidity of statement, all fused with an incomparable power to bring palpitating life out of the dust of old records. I shall never forget the passionate fervor with which, in my youth, I devoured *La Cité Antique,* or how, under the charm of its brilliancy and solidity, I felt a love of history born in me.

If the historian wishes to vitalize past centuries, he must be able to explain human actions in terms of the eternal instincts whereby men are moved; and consequently he must have a profound knowledge of the human soul. In this respect historical and psychological imagination are akin. There are, however, essential differences between them. The former, restricted by the very nature of its subject-matter, is often confined to mere re-creation of actual occurrences, the only elements presented with any certainty in the obscure language of the documents. It is only with infinite precautions that it can risk the interpretation of causes. Psychological imagination, on the other hand, because it progresses commensurately with literary invention, sees a limitless field of construction and hypothesis opening out before it. That is why it ventures boldly beyond human actions in order to analyze the sentiments at the back of them and to note the echoes those actions awaken in our hearts. Wherefore this kind of imagination fully deserves the epithet "psychological." Its aim is to represent those moods which are the obscure reactions of the personality as influenced by circumstance. Its gaze is along the vistas of the spiritual as opposed to the material life—vistas as absorbing as the most variable sky, the most diversified landscape. They are made up of experiences, emotions, memories, and impressions, all garnered subconsciously, stored latent in the recesses of the mind until awakened by some sudden shock which recombines them, thus creating an inner life so intense that it may have all the appearance of reality. This is the characteristic difference between this sort of imagination and other sorts. In lyric, plastic, or fantastic imagination we can clearly perceive the distance which separates the created image from the fragments of truth of which it is composed; in psychological imagination the illusion is so vivid, the creation so perfect, that it is often impossible to say what is invention and what reality.

We have always had a bent toward the study of the human mind; we might even maintain that this sort of imagination has persisted throughout our literature, from the subtle allegories of the *Roman de la Rose* to the exhaustive analyses of a modern novelist such as Paul Bourget. I am going to give you some characteristic examples of this bent as exemplified in different literary modes.

Racine may be regarded as a type of the imaginative psychologist who found in the theater his means of expression. It is no exaggeration to say that his dramatic quality is due solely to his gift of creating emotional situations in his fancy and of seeing them with his mind's eye as clearly as Victor Hugo could photograph with his physical vision the gorgeous pageant of living forms and colors; whence the paucity of action in his plays, as well as the fact that his aim in writing tragedies was to "create something out of nothing."[15] To him, dramatic action consisted in the uninterrupted display of emotions which arose in his own mind and were transmitted to his characters, involving them in a violent conflict between instinct and passion which is his sole device for propelling the dramatic problem toward its solution. And in this way he succeeded in giving his works an intense vitality—the vitality of the human heart.

Stendhal possessed somewhat similar qualities; but he devoted them to the service of the novel. Under a style of almost mathematical precision which might be deemed non-existent to any appeal of the imagination, not only was the author of *Le Rouge et le Noir* hypersensitive, but he was also gifted with the faculty of picturing to himself at will what he "called 'interiors' of the soul." "I meditate endlessly on what interests me," he said in *La Vie d'Henri Brulard,* which is his autobiography, "and by looking at it from different points of my soul I finally descry new things in it and modify its aspect." This significant remark shows us how his psychological vision was formed. When he was absorbed in the observation of the inner life, Stendhal seemed to have attained to a state of veritable ecstasy—the imaginative state *par excellence,* with all functions in abeyance save a certain mental exaltation which allows the mind entirely to lose itself in the contemplation of its object. Stendhal was able thus to create a teeming multitude of emotional visions and experiences of the heart, out of which he composed his characters with such minute care that we almost forget the poverty of their physical life, often reduced to a dangerous minimum.

My third and last example is Sully Prudhomme. It is customary to group the author of *Justice* and *Bonheur* among the philosophic poets. But the same man whose ambition it was to introduce more intellectuality into lyric poetry than it usually contains, wrote also *Les Vaines Tendresses* and *La Vie Intérieure*. And it is when he opens his heart to us, when consequently he is most himself, that we can best study the working of his imagination. A soul, tormented by an incurable melancholy, he was all his life harassed by the effort to reëstablish a moral equilibrium upset by the weight of his doubts. And in the course of the struggle between his desperate longings and his intellectual revolts he stirred into being a complete inner world peopled with emotions, sentiments, and impressions. If he escaped from this morbid introspection in order to seek consolation or a solution of his problems in the outside world, it was never for long. He soon withdrew into himself, and was content to scrutinize the stirrings and record the griefs of his own troubled soul. Gazing into the gloomy lake of his memory, he searched its depths until from the troubled waters there slowly arose the ghosts of his sufferings, hopes, and regrets—

Et dans mon âme illuminée
Seul je descends avec amour.

"Ouvre-toi, Sésame!" La porte
Aussitôt roule sur ses gonds.
J'entre et j'appelle; à ma voix forte
Mon peuple innombrable m'escorte,
Sombres pensers et rêves blonds.[16]

And down into my lighted soul
Alone, rejoicing, I descend.

"Open Sesame!" The door
Swings upon its hinges back.
I enter and aloud implore:
Throng then my people—all the corps
Of golden dreams and brooding black.

IMAGINATION

Never did fresco appear more gorgeous or more animated than this troop of the familiar spirits of the heart's silent places, called to a semi-corporeal existence by the magic wand of poetic inspiration.

The example of Sully Prudhomme attests the charm which the psychological imagination may possess. It is less remarkable for energy than for depth; and the most appealing adjunct to its depth is its delicacy. If it does not move us violently, as the lyric or the plastic imagination does, at least it has an inestimable emotional value in the satisfaction yielded by the sense of deep penetration into unexplored recesses of mind and soul. It is yet another way of escaping everyday life, of reaching the secret haunts of poetry itself.

It has, too, the ultimate degree of refinement. The alternative type of imagination, which recognizes only the phenomena of the outside world, is, after all, primitive, closely allied to mere sensation. It sprang up readily in uncivilized times. It "gave rise to myths, religions, legends, epic and war-like tales."[17] For "young races are like young men: free development is natural to them, as is the simple exuberance of fancy—they see reality as in a fairy tale, transformed by the magic wand of imagination. And so, in the dawn of a nation's literature we find epic and lyric poetry, which sees human life with the enchanted eyes of exaltation."[18] It is only later, when the mind apprehends the joys of pure speculation, that it feels the birth of a desire to curb its instinctive impulses. This is what Macaulay meant when, in his celebrated essay on Milton, he stated that, as civilization advances, poetry almost necessarily declines. In actual truth, poetry does not decline, for it is an ever-living need of the human soul; but it becomes less instinctive, more intellectual.

This is doubtless why psychological imagination is nowadays so peculiarly dear to us. We appreciate, indeed, the writers who are gifted with plastic imagination—Victor Hugo, Théophile Gautier, Lamartine, Zola, and their like—but incontestably there are moments when this kind of imagination does not satisfy a generation so persistently self-analytical and complex as ours. Victor Hugo, however much we may admire him, sometimes offends our sensibilities—and precisely when he is most inspired. We say of him that he is *"peuple,"* meaning that he has a somewhat common way of expressing emotion—a way more attuned to simple than to cultivated minds. We find in such writers as Racine, Stendhal, and Sully Prudhomme a delight at once deeper and more delicate. For their order of imagination answers to the very complexity of our own organization; it reconciles the opposing forces which contend in us; it marks the point at which the two contradictory influences which divide our nature find their equilibrium—on one side the Celtic temperament with its poetical outbursts, its craving for mystery; on the other the Latin, with its ideal of reason and love of balance. It is in very truth the synthesis of our divergent natures—the quintessential expression of the French mind.

V

Sentiment

AS I told you in my first chapter, the Frenchman is an infinitely complicated being. And already I have, I think, fully justified this assertion. You can see for yourselves how in all circumstances, even in the most trivial acts of our life, different and often contradictory tendencies vie for dominion in our minds. Their contention lends its ardor to our individuality and makes it the richer. But it also helps to obstruct the clear perception of this same complexity. For the momentary triumph of one element of our nature does not necessarily imply that that element is the only one which has a decisive influence on our behavior. Such a triumph generally hides inner conflicts, the effects of which are felt even when not seen. And that is why it is so difficult to judge the Frenchman according to appearances or from isolated evidences. Very often the outer manifestations are but a mask for deeper and more essential realities.

Of nothing is this principle more true than of our emotions. We are temperamentally sensitive almost to excess. The natural excitability on which I have already had occasion to comment predisposes us to respond to every impression; we are apt to feel all emotions with peculiar acuteness. We are easily moved; and when for one reason or another we give free rein to our impulses, the result is sometimes startling. Consider, for example, the second half of the eighteenth century. One day, wearied of long years of intellectual tyranny, the French people undertook to kick over the traces (if you will forgive the phrase). Following Rousseau's example, they stood up for the rights of sentiment. From that moment, to be a man of sensibility was to possess all the virtues, to live the full life. "Sensitive beings live more deeply than others," said Duclos; "for them good and evil are multiplied."[1] Accordingly, sensibility was allowed to develop unchecked. People became intoxicated with enthusiasm; they actually courted the anguished throbs of passion. Tears, hitherto regarded as a weakness (witness La Bruyère's saying, "How is it that we laugh at the theater and are ashamed to cry there?"), were shed "in torrents," to use an expression of the time. Comedy itself became pathetic with Nivelle de la Chaussée, and under the pen of Diderot turned into bourgeois drama, reeking with sensibility. Ardent and exalted love took possession of the novel and breathed a subtle spell from every page of *La Nouvelle Heloïse*.

This unleashing of the passions lasted for more than fifty years and was at its extreme when the Revolution broke out. Its effects were still perceptible during the first half of the nineteenth century. At bottom, romanticism was very largely the literary exploitation of sentimentality. For a long time emotion was a sacred thing, and from pure force of habit its rights remained unchallenged. One could even behold men like Scribe, the author of innumerable gay comedies, abandoning themselves to sentiment in their private lives. We know from

SENTIMENT

what Legouvé says that the author of the *Bataille de Dames* was moved to tears with extraordinary ease. "Here is a man," he said, "whom people would not accuse of sentimentality! Well, Scribe could not read, relate, or compose a touching scene without crying. I can still see him, when he read *Adrienne Lecouvreur,* wiping his glasses ten times during the fifth act because they were dimmed with his tears. One day when we were both occupied in sketching out some pathetic scene or other, he threw himself down, clasped my knees, and, kissing my hands, burst out weeping."[2]

This, with all deference to Legouvé, is sentimentality pure and simple. But such extravagance is instructive. It shows us how tender the Frenchman is by temperament, and how his emotions, when given full play, can surpass in intensity those of other peoples who, rightly or wrongly, have a reputation for being more tender-hearted. But I hasten to add that similar examples, although they reveal some of the most secret depths of our nature, are rather rare. To-day, at any rate, we consider the manifestations of feeling to which the eighteenth century gave way as denoting a lack of self-restraint of which we are a little ashamed, and which we should prefer to hide.

In general, our attitude is very different. The Frenchman, especially the cultivated Frenchman, does not like to show the innermost feelings of his heart. When he is moved, he stiffens and tries to disguise his emotions under an air of indifference. Mr. Barrett Wendell had a very delicate appreciation of this trait when he said: "And yet all the while, when I was with these French friends . . . I was aware, even when they were talking most freely with one another, of something more like restraint than would normally have characterized such a company in America. It was not easy to define. It was not reserve, yet it had some touch of reserve. It seemed based on a deep, impulsive, instinctive sentiment that the innermost truth of personal feeling could not decently be revealed—that such truth should be kept sacred for occasions almost of confession, devout or mundane, as the case might be. To unveil it, as we might unveil it at home, I sometimes came to fancy, would have seemed to them like some shameless exposure of spiritual nudity. I can find no better name for the trait I am trying to define than an instinctive modesty of the spirit. Indefinite, elusive, though this peculiarity be, in its teasing contrast with their voluble frankness concerning other matters than spiritual, there can be no doubt that something of the sort is deeply characteristic of the French. However infelicitously I may have explained it, I am sure that it is there to explain. I am sure, too, that one must understand it sympathetically, no matter how little one can articulately define it, before one can fairly understand the mutual misapprehensions which have so long obscured the personal intercourse of the French with their neighbors, the English, or with us of America."[3]

In this passage, the hesitating circumlocutions of which plainly show the author's difficulty in defining an impression peculiarly hard to put into words, I want particularly to accent one phrase: "It would have seemed to them like some shameless exposure of spiritual nudity." These words express admirably what every Frenchman feels when he is obliged to

SENTIMENT

reveal the inner depths of his being. Actual shame, a sort of emotional chastity, holds us back at the verge of avowal and renders it impossible for us to unveil our secret hearts. It seems to us that it would be desecration to throw open the temple of our affections to all comers, and we at once draw a veil between ourselves and strangers, and sometimes even between ourselves and our nearest and dearest. Stendhal is a rather striking example. He was himself the most impressible of men. He could not hear a sad word uttered by the veriest stranger, recall a cherished memory, be present at a touching ceremony, without weeping. But the more he was beset by emotions, the more he stiffened, hiding his weakness under the appearance of coldness and even of hardness. He wrote to a friend: "My feelings have become too acute. Things that touch others only very slightly cut me to the quick. I was like this in 1789. I am still the same in 1840. But I have learned to hide it all under an irony which is unnoticed by the common herd."[4] In his autobiography he said again: "I was never able to speak of what I loved best; such talk would have seemed blasphemy to me."[5] And Balzac expressed the same aversion in well-nigh identical terms. In 1843 he wrote to Madame Hanska: "Never since I was born have I confused the thoughts of my heart with those of my mind, and except for a few lines that I wrote for your eyes alone . . . I have never expressed anything that was near my heart. It would have been the most abominable sacrilege. . . . And so, never point out to me as a rule of conduct in love matters what I may have written. What I have in my heart will never be expressed, and will obey the heart's laws alone."[6]

Mingled with this spiritual modesty is another feeling—one of a more intellectual, less instinctive order—which also does its part toward making it difficult for us to express our sentiments freely. I mean the fear of letting our passions dominate us. We would gladly adopt for our motto the phrase which Madame de Lafayette ascribed to the Princess de Clèves: "I admit that passion may lead me, but it cannot blind me.'" We deem it unworthy of human nature to follow the uncensored prompting of whatever is most instinctive in us; it is, we hold, a proof of mediocrity to "desire nothing except what is dictated by passion," as Descartes put it. In fine, in the sphere of our sentiments there is something analogous to the phenomena which I have already traced in connection with our imagination. We take refuge in intelligence as in the only faculty which can enable us to find a way through the labyrinth of our instincts; we ask the mind to check the wild and irregular throbbings of the heart, to strengthen it in its frailty. Here again, we strive to impose the clarifying processes of reason upon the incoherent fits and starts of emotion.

This decisive intervention of reason in the concerns of the heart has strongly influenced the French conception of love. We have always interfused with passion a spiritual element. It must not be forgotten that it was in France that *l'amour courtois,* chivalrous love, had its origin. You all know its principles and its procedure. In the cult of woman, as conceived and sung by the Provençal poets, love lost every vestige of sensuality. It was the act of adoration of one being kneeling before another whose perfection and nobility were the essential conditions of her

SENTIMENT

sway. And in this quest of an object which must be, above all, perfect, passion (which can easily become the most materialistic of all emotions) was transformed, in the cult of the troubadours, into a craving of mind and soul. "If we analyze the elements contained in this original form of love whereby the Provençals enriched literature," says M. Lanson, "we find that it rests on the idea of perfection conceived as dominating both the intelligence and the will, becoming a goal as well as an experience; and also on the disinterested preference which holds that self should be subordinated to the good of the loved object, according to the degrees of perfection that the lover finds in himself and in the object. Thus the intellectual and moral elements dominate in chivalric love."[8]

Many centuries have passed since the Middle Ages. A hard materialism has ruthlessly imposed its destructive beliefs on the modern world. The conception of chivalric love, alas, is no longer possible. And yet something of its essence, like a far-away perfume from those bygone days, still lingers in the impulses which, in France, inspire love between man and woman. Our most subtle painter of womankind, M. Paul Bourget, noted this persistence among us of the cult of the *"Dame"*: that is to say, of one who is a "superior and adorable being, the object of our steadfast faith and our ever-present help in trouble —she who spurs us to energy in our endeavors and consoles us in calamity; she from whom emanate all gentleness and all nobility, and who can without blasphemy be called an angel. Sentimental phraseology is here no more than the popular expression of a dream which is universal."[9]

Do not misunderstand me. I do not mean that we are insensible to physical attraction. We are a people of too artistic tastes not to desire beauty wherever it may be found, and especially in its most moving form—human beauty. Nor do I assert that bestiality is unknown in France; man is the same everywhere. But here it is a question of degree. A Frenchman who yielded solely to the attraction of the senses in the choice of a loved one would undoubtedly be despised; nay, he would be the first to despise himself. He would be ashamed to become attached to a fool, were she the most beautiful woman in the world. What he desires first and foremost is a certain perfection, either moral or intellectual. If he had to choose between the most dazzling beauty joined to mediocrity of soul, and the superiority of a mind united with physical plainness, he would not hesitate: he would choose the second. And the same is even more true of the Frenchwoman. When, in her girlhood's dreams, she conjures up visions of the future, what she sees is a life in intimate harmony with a man who shares her thoughts and tastes; a man whose success or whose superiority of mind she can admire. She rarely imagines her Prince Charming as a handsome young man whose physical attractions are his only good quality. And when she has found the one with whose life she consents to unite her own, she does not extol him to others by saying, "He is a handsome man!" She praises his intellect, the delicacy of his feelings, possibly the brilliancy of his conversation. She will mention with pride the promises for the future which all these qualities give, and the esteem in which others hold his talents.

SENTIMENT

Let me tell you, as an example, a true story. We will call the heroine, for the purpose of the tale, Suzanne. She was a girl of great beauty—that rather cold and statuesque beauty which is often seen in Frenchwomen. Tall, with regular features, well built, she had in her bearing just a trace of haughtiness. She was remarkably intelligent, too—not very cultivated, but very witty and able to hold her own in the most subtle conversation.

These gifts must have been natural to her, for she had been badly educated. Her parents belonged to a class of people which is to be encountered in all the capitals of the world—a species of high-class adventurers, who manage somehow to maintain the appearance of respectability through the most precarious vicissitudes. The father had formerly, according to his own story, been worth millions. He succeeded in supporting a style of life which distantly recalled his past splendors, but only by a succession of expedients the exact details of which I never knew. The mother lived on her reputation, which was that of a former beauty; and it was her task to arrange the *mise-en-scène* of the household—the only real thing about a family life which was in other respects one perpetual lie.

Suzanne seemed perfectly at ease in these surroundings. She followed the useless round of that cosmopolitan society in Paris which brings together persons of the most dubious character—shady financiers and all the *viveurs* of the globe who expect to find in our capital the El Dorado of self-indulgence. She was the queen of all the fashionable gatherings, and she seemed to look forward to no other destiny than to shine at parties, to show herself in a box at the opera, to see all the young men crowding around her at a ball. She had an undisputed success, and the grace of her beauty, coupled with her wit, provided her with a court of adorers whose eagerness was anything but displeasing to her.

Among all these, there was one who stood out from the others. M. C. was the typical handsome young man—tall, slender, and, though apparently lacking in strength, of a supple vigor methodically kept in training by regular physical exercise. When he entered a drawing-room he was the cynosure of all eyes, so much nonchalant grace and aristocratic poise was there about him. As often happens with the devotees of sport, he was not too well endowed with brains; one might say that he had only that minimum of intelligence which is indispensable to every man who professes cultivation. But, having been brought up by a very intelligent mother who had devoted herself to his education, he supplemented the deficiencies of his mind by a social grace, a knowledge of the world, and an innate gift for conversation which misled nearly everybody. As he happened in addition to be very rich, society was extremely tolerant of his little weaknesses. He paid Suzanne assiduous attention, and it was not difficult to see, from the ecstatic way in which he listened to the girl when she talked, that he was much in love. Suzanne, on her side, showed a distinct preference for her admirer, and I would have wagered that I could infallibly predict the outcome of the story (a story which, so far, had been very commonplace), and with the more assurance because the mother did her utmost to encourage the match. She might have posed as the model for Mrs. Light in Henry James's

SENTIMENT

Roderick Hudson. Like her American sister, she dreamed of reëstablishing her fortune by some brilliant marriage for her daughter, on whom all her hopes were set; and here was a match which would give her both social connections and riches. She almost literally threw herself upon her prey.

It was then that a chance meeting at a watering-place caused the entrance upon the scene of another person—one whose appearance was to overthrow all these plans and calculations. M. G. was an utter contrast to M. C. Shy, retiring, rather under the middle height, with narrow shoulders and a stoop, he was one of those men who pass unnoticed. During the greater part of the year he lived on his country estate in Anjou, whence he drew a modest income. In this secluded life he had cultivated reflective habits which had developed an authentic poetic gift. He was without ambition: he had never even dreamed of publishing any of his poems, although they showed an exquisite feeling of a sort which often reminded me of that delicate writer—our Wordsworth—J. de Pomairols.

Whether we are naturally attracted to natures opposite to our own, or whether, through that peculiar clairvoyance which sensitive and refined natures have in common, M. G. divined in Suzanne a serious nature hidden under a frivolous exterior, I do not know. I do think, however, that something made him want to save the girl from her surroundings. In any event, he immediately fell in love with Suzanne; and somehow, in spite of his shyness, he managed to show her what he felt.

I confess that at this moment all perspicacity abandoned me. I never for a minute supposed that this young man, endowed with the qualities most useless in Suzanne's world, would have the least chance with the acknowledged belle of Parisian drawing-rooms. Imagine how great was my surprise when, two or three months after the events just related, the development of which I had followed with amused interest, I received a letter from Suzanne telling me of her engagement to M. G. I felt that, having known her from childhood, I could ask her to confide in me. And one day she confessed, with a reticence mingled with a glimmer of shame for her earlier frivolity, that she had found out that M. C. was a nonentity whose merits were all on the surface, whereas, as a result of her talks with M. G., she realized that she herself was deepening and maturing. She had felt her intelligence expanding; she had discovered new depths of soul of which she was ignorant; and she had concluded that the possibility of other similar gains was well worth the renunciation of those worldly successes the vanity of which she had now perceived.

Suzanne is to-day, at barely thirty, the mother of four children whom she is bringing up herself. She lives the year round on her husband's country place in Anjou, and is seen in Paris only once or twice a year, staying there just long enough to keep in touch with the artistic and literary affairs which are now her principal satisfaction, and in perfect communion of ideas with her husband, who is more given up to poetry than ever. I met her a short time ago; and when I asked her, "You regret nothing?" she answered, "Nothing!" with a clear look, full of the moral strength of self-knowledge. "I am absolutely happy. I can't understand how I could ever have lived another kind of life.''

Is not this story significant—all the more significant because the ending was unexpected? Here was a young girl who seemed irremediably spoiled by her education, and who, condemned to judging things by appearances only, might have been expected to remain oblivious of loftier ideals. But nature was too strong. Slowly accumulated habits, the heredity of centuries, had kept alive in her a way of feeling which, almost in spite of herself and in spite of obstacles raised by parents unmindful of their duty, had ranged her on the side of what I consider to be the typical Frenchwoman.

The French conception of love which I have just described will now enable you, I think, to understand better what a French marriage is. Probably no French custom is more falsely interpreted by foreigners. We are absolutely astounded when we learn what ideas are prevalent on this subject. According to the most widespread opinion, marriage with us is simply a business proposition. The parents of the future couple meet, determine the sum which each of the parties shall contribute, and, without even consulting the tastes of the two persons most interested, sign the agreement which decides the future of their children. Then, one fine day, the young lady is brought face to face with a young man whom she scarcely knows; and after a few weeks' acquaintance under a strict chaperonage which prevents all intimate conversation, she has to marry him, willy-nilly.

This legend is a monstrous distortion of customs wholly misunderstood. It originated in old narratives embodying the snap-judgments of travelers who had only the most sketchy acquaintance with our habits of life. Things may have happened so in the old days—in the time of Louis XIV—and in the families of the blood royal when dynastic interests and duty to the country took precedence over the personal leanings of the princely couple. And yet, did we not see a granddaughter of Henri IV, the Grande Mademoiselle, fall in love with a penniless younger son and marry him against the king's will? In France, as everywhere else, love is, I assure you, held to be indispensable in marriage. If, sometimes, —as in every country,—considerations of worldly interest are insidiously mingled with the tenderer emotions, we do as the rest of the world does: we try to persuade ourselves that we are guided by love alone, and, lacking the thing itself, we must have at least the illusion. You would very much surprise a young Frenchwoman if you were to assert before her that it is otherwise. Like the English or American girl, she sees in marriage only the realization of a beautiful dream of love.

We do, however,—because our love, as I have shown you, is almost always tempered by spiritual aspirations,—admit that wisdom and experience should logically have their say in estimating realities so delicate as community of tastes and intellectual affinity. Hence the rôle played by the parents— a rôle, moreover, recognized and made almost obligatory by law. The parents are not, as is too readily believed, merchants arranging a financial transaction with their children for counters: they are wise mentors whose office it is to give counsel which the inexperience of the betrothed pair could not formulate without help. It is their duty to ascertain that the passion which the young people believe they feel is based on solid foundations—that it is not merely an illusion which a few years will dissipate, leaving husband and wife face to face with hard reality. They may even play a more active part and guard against the whims of chance. When they see two young persons who seem as if made for one another, because they are in that condition of moral, intellectual, and social equality which is a sure guarantee of sympathetic understanding in the life in common, they discreetly encourage the birth of reciprocal feelings. They arrange "accidental meetings." A stay at the seaside, a party, a dinner—such are the innocent subterfuges which assist fate. At twenty, when the tastes are similar, it is astonishing how quickly love is kindled in two young hearts which have not felt its sway before! What harm is there in that? Is it not a ruse practiced in every country—even in the English-speaking ones, if one is to judge by the existence of the word "matchmaker"? Assuredly nobody will pretend that in such a matter it is preferable to let chance work in its own way. It is better to avoid mistakes than to allow life to inflict its cruel lessons.

The system, we must admit, is not perfect. Not all marriages arranged under the ægis of experience turn out well. Mistakes are committed, for the eyes of the parents are not always capable of discovering the rift in the lute, which inevitably widens until the music of illusion is heard no more. Worldly old men, too, may be more prudent than wise, and may attach more importance to advantages of fortune than to those of character; it is a human weakness. But we can say with all candor that these errors, luckily, are not numerous. In general the parents are sincerely working for their children's happiness. And their love inspires them to judicious choices. All in all, thanks to our marriage custom, we reduce to a minimum those ill-assorted unions, blindly rushed into by mere children, which bring such bitter regrets in their train. We have succeeded in putting that grave problem, marriage, under the sway of reason; and it is an achievement of which we may be justly proud.

Again, it is to the guidance of reason that we confide our pity when it is translated into charity or benevolence. Compassion for our fellow men is perhaps, of all the manifestations of human feeling, the one most easily blinded. The spectacle of human suffering appeals to the most spontaneous and uncalculating of our emotions; and our hearts, taken by surprise, give themselves before we have ascertained whether the impulse of kindness was justified. Thus it comes to pass that the love of our neighbor is so often exploited by hypocrisy or guile.

We have no use for this kind of undiscriminating pity. Turgot, the great French organizer, expressed our common conviction when he said, "The questions of public good must be treated firmly, quietly, without coldness on the one hand, and without sentimentality on the other, but with that heart-felt warmth which results from a profound feeling of justice and love of order."[10] It is on this principle that we have established the most thoroughgoing system of relief in the world. For France is the country which has carried the organization of charity to its highest development. Here again we have to destroy a very widespread fallacy. People accuse us—and many ill-informed French people are, I must admit, among those who spread the error—of being behind other peoples in the matter of social service. But when this verdict is pronounced, two very nearly related but nevertheless quite different things are being confused: private charity and organized charity. As for the many individuals ready and eager to devote themselves to alleviating distress, and the great number of philanthropists giving great sums of money at the dictation of their own impulses, who in a country like America provide so heartening a spectacle and illustrate so wonderful a spirit of generosity, I admit that they are not to be found in France. But if individual charity is less in evidence among us, that is because the organization of public charity is sufficiently well developed and careful in administration as actually to leave but little for private initiative to do.

This is a particular in which we reap the fruits of a long experiment, a system perfected by centuries of trial. The administration of charity in France goes back almost to the origin of our nation. As early as 511, under Clovis, the first Council of Orléans ordered that a part of the revenues of the church should be set aside to succor the poor. Another council, that of 549, provided for visiting the prisons every month and for alms to the lepers. This same council confirmed the establishment of the hospital of Lyons, founded by Childebert and his wife. The hospitals of Saint-Julien-le-Pauvre in Paris, and those of Rheims and Auxerre, also date from this epoch. Before the end of the following century every city had its hospital, and Paris had several. Under Charlemagne these institutions had become so important that it was necessary to group them under various categories of relief: the poor, the sick, orphans, the aged, children. The Emperor, moreover, ordered his vassals to attend to the sick, and he himself took the orphans and the widows under his protection.[11] The organization of relief for foundling children dates from the eleventh century. The first buildings for this purpose were established at Montpellier in 1070 by the Fathers of the Order of the Holy Ghost; the next at Marseilles in 1158.[12] This institution still exists and is connected with the Ministry of Public Relief.

The first legislation concerning the tax to be levied on dramatic amusements, known under the name of *Droit des pauvres,* goes back as early as Charles VI; and the custom itself is probably even older. These laws, still in force, assure to the needy a part of the money which the more fortunate spend on their pleasures.

In 1612 a physician, Théophraste Renaudot, conceived the idea of giving free consultations in Paris —the earliest form of the free clinics of our own day. The same philanthropist instituted an employment office for the poor. This work grew so rapidly that a decree of the Council gave to Renaudot in 1618 the title of General Commissioner of the Poor of the Kingdom. Soon the entire medical profession devoted itself to this good work for the destitute and the suffering. On the 13th of May, 1694, the Parliament gave its approval to these enterprises by formulating a police ordinance regulating medical assistance to the poor, visits to their houses, and free distribution of medicines.[13]

SENTIMENT

It would take too long to enumerate all the efforts in the same direction which have marked the continuous progress of our legislation for more than thirteen centuries, each effort recording some development of public opinion, and all of them bringing constant amelioration and tending to a more and more completely systematic regulation of French charity. If in its inception charity was principally inspired by religion and sprang from an emotional impulse, there was such a lack of coördination among its various activities that the tendency was to transform the spontaneous accomplishment of these duties into an obligation regulated by law; and this tendency grew stronger from the end of the sixteenth century until the day when it was legalized by the centralizing genius of Napoleon, at which time public relief took its place among the regular departments of national administration.[14]

This way of considering charity as the business of all, not merely of a few, has become so integral with our life that even private organizations cannot avoid linking themselves more or less closely with the state organizations, and they inevitably become part of the machinery for administering public charity. A few years ago, for example, there was founded by President Casimir Périer the Alliance of Social Hygiene, which unites in one organization all the agencies, public and private, which deal with the relief of poverty and the betterment of the social order. The aim of this union is to facilitate the division of the work, to coördinate efforts, and above all to avoid any loss of energy in apportioning to the best interests of all the considerable sums devoted to the fight against poverty. So there is working to-day in France a perfected machine the power of which can be felt in the most distant outlying parts of the country. It comprehends in its complicated mechanism every department, town, and individual, and it affects every form which human compassion can take—hygiene, relief to women and children, aid to the sick, the poor, and the aged, accident insurance, societies for the prevention of vice, and many others.[15] Its operation is so efficient that no real misfortune can escape the collective efforts of the entire nation's compassion.

This system of organization, if carried to extremes, has its drawbacks. I deplore the effect which it has of benumbing in us the very feeling which it is designed to express. Anonymous charity necessarily loses some of its ardor; it is deprived of its greatest stimulus, the satisfaction of seeing oneself in one's own works. And the same might be said of all French sentiments. The constant intervention of reason in the affairs of the heart cannot but curtail spontaneity and simplicity of expression. From reflecting too much on our feelings, we run the risk of seeing them grow cold. But there are compensating advantages. Is it, after all, really possible to be good without conscious exertion of the intelligence? I have never seen any beings more radically cruel than fools are, in spite of their sudden impulses of sentimentality. At all events, it is undeniable that intelligence, by throwing light on our instincts, helps us to master them; and to master them is to place them in the service of good. "Conquered passions," said Pascal, "are virtues. Avarice, jealousy, anger —these are attributes possessed even by God."[16]

And, surely, to be able to analyze one's impulses is often to purge them of their natural brutality—to purify and refine them as mere sentimentality could never do.

I wish, in closing, to cite one illustration of what I have in mind. It was related by a Swiss writer, Mme. Noëlle Roger, who worked during the war in our hospitals, and who collected her observations in an extremely pathetic book, *Les Carnets d'une Infirmière*. One day, during a reconnaissance, a French patrol found four seriously wounded Germans dying of hunger. The French, full of compassion, offered them their rations. Three of the wounded accepted and devoured what was given them. The fourth made a sign that it was of no use. Then "the youngest Frenchman, a boy of twenty . . . very sad at not being able to give him anything, went up softly, knelt down, and kissed his enemy on the forehead. The touch of the hairless cheek and the soft lips brought the ghost of a smile to the dying face. The little French soldier had hit upon a way to conjure up beside this death-bed a loved presence, a woman's tenderness—perhaps a mother's face."[17]

You see the rare quality of the emotions which prompted the young Frenchman to this deed of pity. How deep must have been the tenderness of one who, through all the daily ghastliness that so blunted men's sensibilities, could keep such a freshness of compassion! And what a knowledge of the human soul must have inspired such a ruse, deliberately aimed at the very heart of the dying man! Think of the understanding, the almost clairvoyant subtlety of that inspiration which told the lad to act the part of the far-away mother or betrothed, to whom, as he had guessed, the last thoughts of the poor fellow were directed! It was the combination of this psychological intuition with sheer intelligence which gave the act its value. It divested his motive of any mere impulsiveness which it might ordinarily have had; and, because it endowed him with a species of second sight, it enabled him to find his way straight to the uttermost spiritual delicacy. Pondering this episode —an inimitable representation in miniature, it seems to me, of the entire universe of noble emotion—I understood as I had never done before what was meant in olden times by the words *"gentillesse française,"* and why from a very early period our country was called, even by her enemies, Sweet France.

VI

The Social Instinct

THERE is an instinct of human nature, an aspiration of the spirit of which France has always been the personification. Ever since she existed, France has been the incarnation of the social instinct." Thus the American critic Brownell[1] expressed himself, and without doubt all of you who have traveled in our country will agree with him. An Englishman might possibly retire from the world, intrench himself in utter solitude, and in that isolation find happiness. He might perhaps be the happier for having no other company than his own. But a Frenchman unable to mingle with his fellows would cease to be a man. His best qualities, for want of use, would become atrophied. He would pine like a fish out of water. Even in a desert, his first idea would be to try to find someone with whom to live. This trait was noticeable during the colonization of America: the French colonists were to be distinguished from those of the other nations by their evident need of keeping together in a neighborly fashion.[2]

Why is it that one notices in France so preëminent a development of sociability, which is, after all, a tendency common to all mankind? Several explanations have been given. According to Frederick Marshall,[3] it is because we have at our disposal a language uniquely adapted to the exchange of ideas.

"That French manners have been in part nursed up to what they are by the direct action of the language in facilitating the extremes of courtesy, is an argument which will generally be admitted." According to M. Fouillée,[4] on the contrary, the causes of our sociability are to be sought in our temperament itself. "The second distinguishing trait of French quickness of feeling is centrifugal or expansive force; this character seems to be principally Celtic. It is, moreover, usual in the sanguine-nervous temperament, which is not introspective, but rather diffusive, communicative, and radiant. One may deduce an important consequence from this fact. Bring together a large number of men having this superabundant quickness of feeling: an action and reaction will of necessity result, with rapidity and intensity; that is to say, sympathy will be quickly established, and all these men will vibrate in unison. The superior development of the social instinct in France has also, no doubt, intellectual and historical causes; but its primary germ seems to us to be this rapid contagion of expansive feelings, in which mutual suggestion is carried to the very highest pitch."

I am tempted to find a great deal of truth in this last explanation; for very early there was found in France what is, after all, the essential manifestation of the social instinct: society life. In the Middle Ages there were the *cours d'amour*. These were not, as has often been believed on the authority of badly interpreted tradition, permanent tribunals before which lovers could carry their differences. They were simply private gatherings at which the guests, knights and ladies, disported themselves at subtle games of wit. There problems were propounded,—above all, sentimental problems,—discussed at length and from every angle, and given solutions. We have here, in fact, an early form of what were later to be called the *salons*.

The *salons*, properly so called, did not appear until the seventeenth century, and the honor of having founded them rests with Catherine de Vivonne, Marquise de Rambouillet. In the house of this great lady, whom her intimates called by the somewhat pretentious name of Arthénice, savants, poets, and fine gentlemen met together; and this was really the first organization of the refined and intellectual classes of fashionable society. Then were established for the centuries to come "the relationships, customs, and habits of life and of mind which characterize the restricted circle formed by the élite of the nation and known to us as 'society.' "[5] The elements contributed were various. Great seigneurs gave the tone, imposed their taste for fine manners; men of intellect propounded philosophy and æsthetics as fascinating topics of speculation; women added the softening influence of their delicacy and subtlety. It was, as Chapelain said, "fashionable society purified," "the touchstone of the gentleman"; and it was also the world of letters made more presentable and, so to speak, tamed. From that day an alliance was achieved between the art of living and intelligence, the one gaining in strength and the other in charm.

Society life, so defined, must have responded to the most profound needs of the French soul, for the *salons* at once multiplied. "The example of the Marquise was imitated everywhere; all over the fashionable Paris of the day, around the Louvre and the Cardinal's Palace, in the Marais and in the Place Royale, the palaces of princes and seigneurs and even the houses of the rich *bourgeoisie* opened their doors. Everywhere there sprang up groups and côteries in which one was constantly meeting intimate friends of like tastes—at the houses of the Marquise de Sablé, Mme. de Maure, Mmes. Clermont d'Entragues, Mme. Paulet, Mme. de Choisy, Mme. Scarron, Mlle. de Scudéry, the Vicomtesse d'Auchy, and Ninon de l'Enclos. . . . The fashion naturally reached the provinces; and soon, from one end of the country to the other, one saw nothing but *salons* in which beautiful and learned ladies cultivated the art of being *précieuses*."[6]

Since those days the fashion has never gone out—a proof that it was not a passing craze, but the expression of a national instinct. Far from waning, the influence of the *salons* only waxed the greater as time went on. In the eighteenth century they became very active semi-philosophical, semi-political centers in which the social future of France was discussed. Mme. de Lambert, Mme. du Deffand, the Maréchale de Luxembourg, Mme. Geoffrin, Mme. de Tencin, Mme. Necker, Mme. Suard, and Mme. Helvétius went wild about the new theories, encouraged, protected, and caressed the philosophers, and made the whole country pay the penalty for playing with fire by setting it ablaze. There was actually seen the spectacle of an actress, Mlle. Quinault, giving harbor to a society, *Le Bout du Banc,* of whom d'Alembert was the idol, and a count—the Comte de Caylus—the humble secretary. The most celebrated of the *salons* in the eighteenth century was unquestionably that of Mlle. de Lespinasse. The extant descriptions of it enable us to picture accurately those "Feasts of Reason" at which the play of wit was so incessant. Mlle. de Lespinasse had been companion or *lectrice* to Mme. du Deffand. But the satellite committed the error of being wittier than her benefactress, and a quarrel ensued. Mlle. de Lespinasse retired, carrying numerous admirers with her—Turgot, the president Hénault, Marmontel, d'Alembert, the Duchesse de Châtillon, Condillac, Condorcet, and others. In her house in the rue de Bellechâsse "she regaled her guests with conversation." "Nowhere," said Marmontel,[7] "was talk more alert, more brilliant, better regulated than at her house. That degree of temperate ardor which she contrived to maintain, sometimes moderating and sometimes stimulating it, was a rare phenomenon. . . . Her gift of launching a thought and then offering it to the men of this stamp for discussion; her gift of discussing it herself as accurately and sometimes as eloquently as they; her gift of introducing new ideas and changing the subject, always with the ease and dexterity of a fairy changing the scene of her enchantments at a stroke of her wand—this gift, I repeat, was that of no ordinary woman."

And neither the Revolution nor the democratization of manners fundamentally changed the make-up of fashionable society in France. After disappearing in the uncertainties which accompanied the great upheaval of 1789, the *salons* reappeared when political calm was restored. Mme. de Staël, Mme. de Genlis, Mme. Récamier, Mme. de Rémusat, Mme. de Beaumont, and Mme. de Girardin were the zealous guardians of this ideal embodiment of refined thinking. And never were the *salons* more numerous or more active than under the Third Republic—a fact of which the best evidence would be the long list which I could compile of the hostesses who knew, or still know, how to gather around them the worlds of literature, art, science, and politics.

As we have noted, what has always characterized the French *salons* and given them distinction throughout Europe is that they were not centers of frivolity dedicated to mere empty diversion. People did not gather together for vain ceremonies, supping, or dancing. They sought, above all, intellectual contact, enrichment through the interchange of ideas.

Thus it was that conversation, the instrument of such interchange, became a necessity of society life in France. Now, the Frenchman was predestined by his very nature to be a past master in the art of speech. I thoroughly agree with Mr. Hart's sally in his book *Understanding the French:*[3] "There are Germans," he says, "who talk when they feel like it. There are Englishmen whom no power on earth can force to talk. But I have yet to discover the Frenchman whom anything short of complete isolation could restrain from talking." The Frenchman is talkative, undoubtedly; and conversation has always been one of his important businesses. Mlle. de Montpensier thought that it was "the greatest and almost the only pleasure of life," and she preferred the Tuileries to the country because "it is more convenient for talking." "Conversation," said Mlle. de Scudéry, "is the social link of all men, the greatest pleasure of gentlefolk, and the most ordinary means of introducing into the world not only politeness but also the purest morals, the love of glory, and the love of virtue."[9]

But we do not—as you can see by the above quotation—talk for the mere sake of talking. We like our conversation to be worth while, to have an educative value. You will find in France, no doubt, as everywhere else, houses in which slander, scandal, and worldly gossip constitute the meager fare of the intellectual entertainment. But the gatherings in which you hear only vain and purposeless twaddle are, for that very reason, reputed to be the meeting-places of fools. We want to get some profit from conversation, by way either of new knowledge or else of some verification or revision of our ideas; we are always aiming at an enlargement of our intellectual horizon. This is what Saint-Evremond meant when he declared that he preferred conversation to reading. And in the same way Varillas admitted to Ménage that out of ten things which he knew he had learned nine by conversation. "I could almost say the same," answered Ménage, who was, as everyone knows, the most learned man of his century.[10]

But the most serious intercourse should never be tedious. We detest pedantry, whatever its disguise. You may discuss a philosophical question, even of the most abstruse kind, but it should be in an agreeable and graceful way and with that lightness of touch which makes it easily understood. To do this, one must know how to say things gracefully, as if in play, and not insist unduly on what is evident to the ordinary intelligence. Nimble wits must be spared the torture of having to think slowly; and more must be left to the understanding than is actually explained. Frederick Marshall said with as much felicity as truth:[11] "No people are so able as the French to imply indirectly what they do not choose to say point-blank. . . . Their words are, for the most part, absolute, but . . . their talk is suggestive rather than declarative, . . . their ordinary disposition in conversation is to convey their meaning by implication and not to give it outright." Above all, talk must never be allowed to degenerate into a monologue or a lecture. Any man who tries to monopolize our attention, be he the greatest genius in the world, deserves brusque treatment; for by doing it he proves his ignorance of the elementary rules of the art of conversation. Probably no people loves eloquence more than we. But speeches have their places in Parliament, in conference halls, at official dinners; apart from these occasions, they are rigorously banished. Rather, the man who knows how to talk well must have the art of repartee—that is to say, the knack of finding a prompt and piquant answer to questions, be they thick as bees from a swarming hive. All of which implies, in the words of Mme. de Staël, "alternating listeners who mutually encourage one another."[12] The seasoned conversationalist is he who, restraining his own desire to shine, knows "how to yield to successors eager for their turn to speak,"[12] and who even contrives to introduce such ideas as will permit others to contribute their own felicities. So managed, conversation is a lively game, in the course of which brilliant or profound sayings pass lightly from mouth to mouth, are seized, and are as lightly flung forth again, only to be caught anew in an incessant exchange of thoughts among the players.

And that is why such conversation inevitably

sparkles with wit. For the distinguishing attribute of wit, wherein it differs very markedly from humor, is that it is engendered only in sympathetic company. I can well imagine a humorist shutting himself up in a morose privacy and distilling his reflections drop by drop, pitilessly analyzing the foibles of men or the illogical aspects of life. But wit perpetrated in cold blood would be as far from the true French spirit as the frothy wine which Germany exported before the war was from clear, limpid, sparkling champagne. It would leave a harsh after-taste such as would at once betray its origin. It would lack the inimitable lightness which arises from the unforeseen contact of ideas captured in mid-flight and volleyed back from the racquet of a supple, ingenious, agile mind.

Two circumstances—the peculiar development of social life in France and the prestige which "society" has always had in the estimation of the rest of the nation—have led to the imposition of certain laws minutely regulating human relationships. In every detail of our lives we apply precepts which have been put to the proof by centuries of usage. From the day of our birth to that of our death, every one of our acts is performed according to certain prescriptions which we cannot ignore without danger of making others suppose that we have thrust ourselves upon a society which our manners give us no right to enter. And we submit to these rules without discussion. That is why the ceremonial which regulates our relationships is so complicated. For everyone takes this code of civility seriously. A dinner party, even in a modest establishment, is given according to the rules of a procedure as studied as that which applies to official receptions at the most meticulous court; the choice of guests is determined upon only after the most anxious reflection; and when the list is settled, what worry and hesitation over the problem of seating the guests according to precedence, age, rank, or merit! On such an occasion the mistress of a house is equal in ingenuity and tact to the most accomplished master of ceremonies at an embassy.

Foreigners are amused by our exaggerated attention to acts insignificant in themselves—acts which might, it would seem, be conducted in a good-naturedly unceremonious way. They think we are very naïve indeed to take so much trouble to make ourselves uncomfortable. And hence they conclude that French civility, because it has consciously become so uselessly meticulous, must be only a narrow formalism, a sequence of mechanical gestures uninfluenced by reason and even less by sentiment. That is certainly judging by appearances alone. To know the usages of good society, to behave in all circumstances as custom ordains, is only the A B C of good breeding. The true French politeness demands something deeper—above all, something that is more the result of reflection, something inseparable from the delicacy of our nature and dependent on the underlying reality of our manners. In France "politeness" has kept its etymological meaning. The polite man is he who has been so polished and softened by life as to have lost the rough edges which would make contact with him unpleasant to others. He is a civilized person who has so completely rid himself of his native uncouthness that he is incapable of hurting his fellow creatures; who can actually sacrifice his own comfort in order to make the life of his neighbor more agreeable. "It seems to me," said La Bruyère,—and in these words he gave the most exact definition possible of this virtue,—"that the spirit of politeness is a certain care to act in such wise that our speech and our behavior shall make others pleased with us and with themselves."[13] It consists, then, in eliminating egotism and in sacrificing oneself for the happiness of others. The truly polite Frenchman, according to La Bruyère's definition, gives a lesson in humility every time he performs a courteous action. For example, Louis XV, the most affable sovereign we have ever had, would "gracefully salute the least important bourgeoise whom curiosity attracted to his path";[14] and by so doing he showed that he knew both how to forget his own rank and also how to give the insignificant bourgeoise the delightful illusion of having been honored by a king. And this attitude of self-effacement was always that of the women who held the celebrated *salons*. Marmontel said of Mme. Geoffrin: "She instituted two regular dinners at her house: one, on Monday, for artists; the other, on Wednesdays, for men of letters. And it is a remarkable fact that, without any knowledge whatever of art or letters, this woman who had never read or learned anything in her life, except in the most cursory way, was not at all at sea in these subjects; she was actually at her ease. But she had the good sense never to speak except about what she knew very well, and in everything else to give way to well-informed persons, always remaining politely attentive herself, without even seeming bored by what she did not understand.

. . ."[15] Legouvé said the same thing of Mme. Récamier and of Mme. de Rauzan, daughter of the Duchesse de Duras: "The art of conducting a salon is a very delicate one. . . . These two ladies possessed the secret because they had the first quality necessary: they were distinguished without being superior. They did not wish to shine themselves, but to make others shine."[16]

Politeness, so conceived, demands a mind always on its guard, a constant care to humor the susceptibilities of the persons with whom one is associated, a continual prevision of the effect of one's words. Sometimes it may even call for real courage. It is related that at the time of the Revolution the Duke of Bedford invited the French duc de G., who was in England, to dine with him. During the meal there was served an old Constance wine which, according to connoisseurs, was delicious. It was praised by the Duke of Bedford, who, to do greater honor to his guest, poured out a glass for him with his own hand. The Frenchman raised the glass to his lips, tasted it, and quaffed it at one draught, replying, when asked by his host, that it was excellent. The Duke of Bedford then started to drink; but at the first taste he uttered an exclamation of disgust. Servants hurriedly examined the bottle and discovered that the butler, by an inexplicable error, had served them castor oil! The French duke had swallowed the appalling drug without wincing. The English admired this action enormously, and "they conceived, it was reported, a very high idea of a country in which courtesy could attain to such heroic proportions." For a Frenchman this act was quite natural: the discovery of the mistake would necessarily distress the host and put him in a ridiculous position, and this the duc de G. had tried to avoid by dissimulating his own repugnance.

At this point I shall propound a question which ought to be answered searchingly, for it touches a matter which is at the root of many misunderstandings of the French character. Up to what point is this consideration for others' susceptibilities compatible with strict sincerity? Does not the desire to please sometimes lead us into embroidering the truth? Is not the Frenchman a notorious flatterer? When an Englishman would not hesitate to speak out brutally, because in his opinion to understate his thought or even to be silent about it would be to tell a lie, is it not the Frenchman's custom to say pleasant things at whatever cost? Certainly there is a modicum of truth in this allegation. When the duc de G. imperturbably declared that the castor oil which he had swallowed was delicious, he was not telling the truth. But to admit so much is a far cry from saying that when a Frenchman tries to be pleasant he is deliberately lying. Often in this country I have praised certain customs or persons with the utmost sincerity, only to hear my interlocutor explain, "Oh, but you French are so polite—!" And the end of the phrase was lost in a gesture which said plainly enough, "We know that you often stretch the truth." I have concluded, perforce, that for you a Frenchman's praise and a lie are almost synonymous. Now, you may believe me when I say that untruth is considered in France with the same reprobation as in the Anglo-Saxon countries. Indeed, one could not insult a man more deeply than to call him a liar. And as for compliments, you must not imagine that they are common coin. To compliment is an art, as is politeness itself. Not everybody is capable of handling praise. The man who ladles out eulogy without tact is forever condemned; he classifies himself at once as a fool. The compliment (for such a thing exists), to be admissible, must be of delicate quality. It does not consist in uttering without rhyme or reason some crass piece of flattery in order to caress another's vanity. It records our perception of some quality of which our interlocutor has a right to be proud, and to which we pay homage. As soon as exaggeration is involved—to say nothing of untruth—the compliment becomes gross flattery and turns against the fool who utters it. Indeed, a compliment paid in good faith is a proof of perspicacity and intelligence; it expresses a profound truth to which it is the speaker's aim to call attention. In the motive behind it we have one more application of the essential principle of politeness as La Bruyère defined it: the effort to make people pleased with themselves and with us.

This analysis shows that true French courtesy is inevitably akin to the tenderness of feeling of which I spoke in my last chapter. It is not pure automatism, as is commonly believed. On the contrary, it presupposes sensitiveness, great kindliness, and a natural delicacy. Bismarck, who certainly did not err on the side of softness, asserted that the French possessed politeness of manners, but knew nothing about the politeness of the heart. That utterance proves that he understood nothing about what he called our manners. Our ancestors were too subtle to have had to wait for lessons from a German. As early as the seventeenth century, La Bruyère, whom

I have so often invoked, had carefully distinguished politeness of mind from politeness of manners.[17] Barthélemy, the author of the *Voyage du Jeune Anacharsis,* had likewise asseverated that the politeness of the heart is far superior to that of manners.[18] And Voltaire himself had indited these lines:

> *La politesse est à l'esprit*
> *Ce que la grâce est au visage.*
> *De la bonté du cœur elle est la douce image,*
> *Et c'est la bonté qu'on chérit.*[19]
>
> As grace is to the outward mien,
> So is politeness to the spirit:
> It is the inner sweetness, which alone hath merit,
> In lovely outward semblance seen.

And, indeed, in this distinction lies the profound value of politeness as it has always been practiced in France.

When all is said, it is because French manners are interwoven with kindliness that one experiences in France so much amiability. All foreigners have noticed it; no country can be found in which the relationships between individuals are more easy or more pleasant. Your great Franklin, who was anything but blind so far as we are concerned, paid us this testimony: "They are the nation with whom it is most agreeable to live . . . the welcome that we get everywhere gives us the highest idea of French politeness. They have the same attentions for a stranger that they have in England for a lady." The most German of Germans have been won by our amenity and forced to bow before its charm. Listen to the confession by Sophie Gutterman, better known under the name of Madame de la Roche: "This affable spirit lessens distances. . . . I am a stranger here; I love the Fatherland. But I am fair-minded, and I recognize that the constant enjoyment of amiability, sociability, gayety, and kindliness makes up one of the best parts of a happy life. This happiness the land of France offers everywhere."[20] And, truly, as soon as one sets foot on our soil it seems as if one began to breathe a benign atmosphere. The very loiterers become alert as soon as they find an occasion to help you. You lose your way, and your anxious look betrays your predicament: ten persons will offer to put you on the right road. An accident happens: a whole crowd takes pity on you and tries to console you. From the greatest to the least, this instinct to help is universal.

The truth is that, in a country in which everyone has contracted the habit, not only of respecting the feelings of his neighbor, but also of considering the well-being of the whole community, the conflict between individuals—that scourge of all societies—is, if not made impossible, at any rate reduced to a minimum. Extreme individualistic tendencies are taught repression; rivalries lose their bitterness. Led by sympathy, people gradually forget their own interests. In this connection one cannot overestimate the effect of a careful observance of forms on the expression of overemphasized individuality.

I want to tell you an anecdote which shows how much moral value there may be in good manners. It is related[21] that Sosthène de la Rochefoucauld, duc de Doudeauville, when very aged, was coming laboriously down the stairs of a house at which he had just made a call, when he met a young man who was bounding up the same stairway three steps at a time. The two men stopped. Following a very laudable custom, they bowed, hat in hand, and each of them stepped aside. Note that the duke, by the prerogative of age, had ten times the other's right to pass first. But he was a man of exquisite politeness, and with a gesture he motioned the young man to continue. No less polite, the latter excused himself. The two remained face to face, with repeated invitations to pass and as many courteous refusals. They might have gone on so indefinitely if the young man had not had a sudden inspiration. He bowed respectfully and said, "I obey, monsieur; obedience is the first duty of youth." Picture to yourself those two human beings, blocked on a stairway and spending precious time in ceremonies: you may find in it an example of a good thing carried to almost childish lengths, and you may smile. But if you smile, you will, in sober truth, be in the wrong. I have just set before you two types very rare in this world: an old man laden with honors, used to everybody's respect, who nevertheless renounces his privileges in deference to his ideal of good manners; and, what is even more admirable, a young man who is not full of his own conceit and who knows what is due to age—two innate egoisms repressed and reduced to silence by the exigencies of good breeding!

A country in which egoism knows self-control must possess the secret of generous ideas. Altruism has been, indeed, one of the characteristics shown in our history. Politeness has made us discover the sweets of philanthropy. Consider what happened in the eighteenth century. It was the time when manners had become refined to a delicacy which they will probably never regain. Never had social life been more exquisite. A combination of elegance and delicacy in human intercourse made existence a sheer delight. "Whoever did not live in the twenty years preceding the Revolution did not know the sweetness of living," said Talleyrand.[22] And it was precisely that time of extreme sociability which saw the birth of those humanitarian ideas by which the following century was inspired. It was everyone's ideal to work for the common happiness; and this happiness was found only in the alleviation of suffering. To whatever excess this passion for solidarity led, its intention was undeniably generous; and one can excuse the excesses in remembering the refined ideal of politeness which was the source of their extravagance.

But French manners have had something more than a civilizing and humanizing influence. Their greatest value has been an element of social consolidation. First of all, they have been useful in determining values. In France everybody has the right to rise. The person of most humble birth can aspire to supreme honors; and when he has reached the summit nobody will remember or question his origin. It has always been thus. Even in the days when an unyielding aristocratic system maintained rigorous class distinctions, a career was always open to talent. All the ministers of Louis XI were self-made men. Voiture, who laid down the law at the Hôtel de Rambouillet and was on equal terms with the greatest in the land, was the son of a wine-merchant of Amiens. Racine, who became gentleman-in-waiting to the king, had for father a mere superintendent of the salt *dépôts*. Colbert, who shared with his king the most absolute power, had begun by selling cloth across a counter. The Paris brothers, great masters of finance under Louis XV, were born in a humble inn at Moirans. And so with others. But natures which are radically vulgar, whatever their power may be, find themselves inexorably debarred from good society. It is in vain that a *parvenu* attempts to take the world of fashion by storm; if he does not prove that he is capable of avoiding with ease and grace the pitfalls which test good breeding, he will be given short shrift. And if he happens to be ill-advised enough to think he can treat people roughly and crush them by the weight of his fortune and his impudence he will soon be put in his place by common consent. I used to know one of these impossible adventurers. He was born at Marseilles in a district swarming with the weird population which is the scum of the port (it faces the Levant, and in it all sorts of flotsam and jetsam come to the surface). Was he even a Frenchman? No one ever knew the facts. One day he disappeared. He had taken his passage on a boat bound for India, and for many years he gave no sign of life. Then he reappeared. He was a millionaire. By what chance—or what crime—had he acquired his immense fortune? That was his secret, and he kept it well; the only thing certain was that riches had been powerless to change his nature. I can see him still—fat and short, with a red face and beady black eyes that were both crafty and stupid, his hairy hands covered with showy rings. I can still hear the guffaws of his thick, vulgar voice. Well, the fellow took it into his head to conquer Parisian society—like a gorilla who, seeing men, wants to imitate them. He made advances, pushed himself, clung desperately to the skirts of society, gave parties of oriental splendor, bought up all the poor fellows who are in the habit of selling their talents, and made them megaphones through which he advertised himself. It was all to no purpose. When people accepted his dinners it was only to laugh at them. At last, one day, a piece of impertinence drew on him a scathing retort from one of the persons whom he had overwhelmed with attentions; and so great was his fury that it brought an apoplectic seizure which put an end to his ambitions. The more I reflect on this story, the more significant it seems to me of the real strength which is the backbone of French society. Our strict guard over our manners is an excellent means of getting rid of the riff-raff which life drags in its train. We have succeeded by this means in conserving under a cloak of equality those necessary distinctions which nature has made between individuals, against which all formulas are powerless, and which are the very condition of the efficient working of all social organizations. In taking for a national ideal a select group which has for its criteria elegance, delicacy, and intelligence, we have formed a good and a sane democracy, which levels up instead of leveling down—in a word, a democracy which aspires to aristocratic perfection.

For it can be maintained that this select group has converted the majority of the nation. In *Understanding the French* one of your compatriots, Mr. Hart, has made a very true remark: "I think a comparison between their manners and ours, taking everything

THE SOCIAL INSTINCT

into consideration, leads to this: although Frenchmen are not more polite, on the whole, than Americans, it is true that more Frenchmen are polite. When you settle down to live in France, what surprises you is the marvellous diffusion of good manners, not the occasional exaggeration of good manners."[23] It is, indeed, surprising to see the ease with which the French assimilate the manners of the most cultivated classes. You may shake hands with a Frenchman who will seem to you a model of distinction, without suspecting for an instant that he is perhaps the son of a peasant and that his father may at that very moment be driving the plough with his horny hands—so well have these "upstarts" (I use the word in a complimentary sense) adopted the gestures, the language, and, best of all, the nobility of soul of the élite.

Are the French eminently adaptable, or should we see in this phenomenon a proof of the irresistible power of habits which, having reigned supreme for centuries, have acquired a particular virtue? There is probably some truth in either explanation. At all events the result is in no degree doubtful. Good manners, imposed and codified by society, constitute in France an imperishable defense and protection of the entire social structure. And the walls of this defense are so strong, and withal so spacious, that everyone can easily be accommodated. We have our revolutionaries, too. By temperament we may even have a sort of taste for personal independence. But those persons are very rare and very intractable who are not influenced by good breeding and irresistibly attracted by urbanity. When by chance some wild spirit takes it into his head to assault the edifice raised by centuries, he is very quickly hypnotized into quiescence by the glamour of good breeding; he calms down, takes off his hat, and submissively assumes his place in the ranks, won over in his turn by the irresistible charm of French politeness and all that it represents.

And that is why, in these days of terrific upheavals, French society remains unshaken. If we are "a people intensely organic and unified,"[24] we owe it in great degree to the rigidity of our social code. We have marched very quickly on the high-road of progress, and in our haste we have sometimes courted dangerous adventures. But through all vicissitudes we have kept our ideal of courtesy and of kindly solidarity. And that has saved us time and time again. It is to this ideal, as much as to any, that we owe our success in having advanced with the times and yet retained whatever of the past was good.

It seems to me that in these matters France offers a wonderful example to a world infected with the virus of anarchy. The phenomenon which will doubtless startle the historians of the future when they study the end of the nineteenth century and the beginning of the twentieth is the spectacle of gradual dissolution which we shall present to their astonished eyes. For mankind is now frenziedly destroying that which century upon century of slow evolution had painfully created—the sense of a strong and strengthening social cohesion. And now that the cataclysm of the Great War has further contributed to the loosening of the bonds, we see the whole edifice crumbling and on the brink of ruin. More than ever do we need to oppose a neutralizing influence to all

THE SOCIAL INSTINCT

these disintegrating forces. So do not mock at traditions which keep order among undisciplined mobs, even if those traditions seem somewhat out of date. Be assured that there is no harm to be feared from the repression of men's instincts; rather, it is the free development of individualism that is fraught with menace. It is because French politeness is a constant check on the natural egoism of man that it is so valuable, and that it forms a most fortunate manifestation of our social instinct. Far from trying to weaken, we should do every possible thing to strengthen it, if, in this shaken world which we have to build anew, we wish to see the reign of peace and good will toward men.

VII

Morals and Family Life

THE aspect to which I am now coming is vital, for it has to do with nothing less than the spiritual health of a nation—the question of morality. Without a delicate feeling for right and wrong, without a high and rigorously served ideal of conduct, a people is nothing but an aggregation of appetites, passions, and instincts—a gangrenous body which must inevitably disintegrate, or which, at the very least, is condemned to a rapid decadence. Now, there is a widely held opinion among foreigners which predicts exactly this lamentable end for France. I do not speak of those of our enemies who go to extreme lengths—those who, veiling their faces with a hypocritical gesture, call down the thunder of heaven upon our corruption. But even our best friends, impressed by all this outcry, admit that we are not so punctilious as good morals would have us be; and, though they sympathize with us and plead all sorts of extenuations, they almost believe in the degeneracy of the French nation.

I admit, moreover, that we do our very best to undermine our own reputation. We are the first to say shocking things about ourselves. To hear us, you would think that everything is going wrong. There is nothing that we do not censure—our habits, customs, manners, administration, politics. We pitilessly disclose our hidden shortcomings and search out our most insignificant weaknesses. Can we wonder if those who listen to our words take all this self-criticism for an account of actual ills?

In this respect we are the victims of a quality which, carried to excess, does us injury. As I have told you, hypocrisy in matters of opinion is unknown among us, and it never enters our heads that anyone could deny the existence of vice. We know that man is not perfect, that nothing is more difficult than to walk in the path of virtue. And we admit it frankly. Some peoples make it a rule never to acknowledge this truth; they live in a fool's paradise and ignore the fact that not the entire human race is ripe for heaven. But the Frenchman asseverates in no uncertain voice that man is a composite of good and evil—and he boldly asserts his own humanity. He does not suppose himself to be any worse than others, but he is certain that he is no better. It is, then, unthinkable that he should pose as virtuous. By admitting that he is human he takes upon himself every human weakness.

And, holding vice to be an undeniable reality, he does not hesitate to speak of it, as of all things which God has made, with an intellectually passionate interest. Hence his conversation seems, to foreigners accustomed to speaking of certain subjects in hushed tones, uncommonly free. And they accuse him of depravity. In point of fact, this freedom of his ought to be the best proof of the innocence of his intentions. What often perverts an idea is the secrecy which surrounds it. Do not American educators believe that the best means of removing the dangerous attraction from sexual subjects is to consider them as natural—that, in losing their mystery, they become innocuous? In France, from time immemorial, we have applied this rule among adults. You may hear the most delicate topics discussed in a drawing-room before women; you will hear these women take part in the debate without the slightest embarrassment. That is because the whole thing is kept in the domain of pure intelligence. It is a question of ideas, and people know it. The most refined person on earth is not besmirched by a discussion which involves only the reasoning faculties. This detachment is another of the aspects which Barrett Wendell understood. During his stay in France, he said, he heard conversations which an Anglo-Saxon would have called shocking; but their whole tone and spirit immediately told him that they were harmless. "To you the situation in question had seemed vividly individual; Armand was Armand, Germaine was Germaine. To them, for all the precision of the terms which set forth the loves of Armand and Germaine, the situation had evidently become generalized. You had been thinking of it in arithmetical terms; to them the terms had rather been algebraic. It is ten to one that where you would have said 'Armand' in discussing the situation, they will say 'a man'; that where you would have said 'Germaine,' they will say 'a woman,' or 'a wife,' or 'an honest woman.' Before you have quite realized this difference, the conversation will very likely have pursued its way still further. It will have generalized itself, you hardly perceive when and how; and these volatile people will be gravely, animatedly, yet dispassionately discussing an abstract problem of psychology, of conduct, of morals. That now and again they revert to a man or a woman, to Armand or Germaine, does not alter the case. What has really interested them, what they will discuss until some more apposite topic distracts them, might just as well have been suggested by a sermon or by an open lecture at the Sorbonne, as by a dramatic performance which had seemed to you, in certain respects, abominable.'"[1]

And it is the same in our literature. (I mean our genuine French literature, not those works which are written for the export trade by goodness only knows whom, and which it is obviously a mistake for our laws to allow under the misapplied principle of freedom of the press.) It cannot be otherwise, for our conversations generally do nothing more than extend the province of the book. In former days this liberty of language was common to all countries. English literature, for example, was in its early stages quite as outspoken as ours. The writers of the Middle Ages related without shame stories which nowadays are considered indecent. The worthy Chaucer, if he were not protected by his archaic vocabulary, would incur the disapprobation of prudish people; and Shakespeare himself spoke of the disorders of the senses in terms the crudity of which makes the most unprejudiced of Frenchmen blush. Neither did the eighteenth century know reticence. And that was well. Nothing could be healthier than the vigorous realism of, for example, a Fielding. It was only in the nineteenth century that the portrayal of certain vices was forbidden in English literature. But in France we have continued to suppose that sexual disturbances are an evil belonging to all time, and that to ignore is not to abolish them. And because we have persisted in frankness when silence was considered more fitting, we have compromised our reputation. This is not a world in which it is discreet to be unlike others; one's voice never sounds louder than when it echoes amid a profound silence. To this day, all that our candor has brought us is the suspicion of having meant our writings to minister to the debased passions of men. And people conclude —not too logically, it may be—that a society in which the delicate situations treated in our novels and plays can occur so often must be hopelessly corrupt.

Now, this supposition—on which are based all the charges of immorality brought against our country—is rendered all the more untrue by the fact that our writers err rather from an excess of moralizing zeal in their motives. French literature has always had an undeniable tendency toward preachifying. Nor am I thinking only of those of our philosophers or essayists who have devoted themselves to the study of human nature in order to draw striking lessons therefrom, such as Montaigne, Charron, La Fontaine, Pascal, Perrault, La Bruyère, La Rochefoucauld, the Montesquieu of the *Lettres Persanes,* the Voltaire of the *Contes,* Vauvenargues, Joubert, and the like; nor yet of the ranks of our writers of sermons, Protestant as well as Catholic—Calvin, Théodore de Bèze, Jean Claude, Bossuet, Bourdaloue, Fléchier, Massillon, Jacques Saurin, Mgr. de Frayssinous, Père de Ravignan, Père Lacordaire, Mgr. Dupanloup, Père Hyacinthe, Père Monsabré, Père Didon, and so on. What I maintain is that *every* French writer is more or less a moralist. "It is a constant trait of the active and positive French mind, from the Middle Ages to our own times, to find difficulty in understanding a work of art, whether literary or plastic, unless it have an utilitarian aim or an edifying or instructive application."[2] Hence that irresistible tendency of ours throughout the Middle Ages to make all literature—drama, poetry, allegory, satire—count toward the education of mankind; hence the preference shown by our Renaissance for those authors of antiquity who provided precepts or examples of virtue; hence the passion of our seventeenth century for psychology, and its desire, not only to study man, but also to make him better by formulating for him a moral code of living.

In the following centuries, even the writers whose works may appear objectionable had a moral purpose, and loudly proclaimed it. In the preface of *Manon Lescaut* the Abbé Prévost said: "The reader will see in the conduct of M. des Grieux a terrible example of the power of the passions. . . . Few of its episodes fail to teach a lesson. . . . The whole work is a moral treatise, agreeably made into a story." The younger Dumas, whose plays so often outrage the prudish among my countrymen—for we have such people— served as spiritual guide for the masses during a good half of the nineteenth century; and one of his defects, clearly, is his inclination to use the stage as a pulpit. We might say as much of Émile Augier. *Sapho,* by Alphonse Daudet, a novel which caused an outcry, is dedicated "To my son, when he reaches the age of twenty"—a clear enough indication of the author's intentions. There is not one of the list —not even Zola, if only we look beyond the ugliness and vulgarity of his pictures—who failed to pursue the vision of a better and purer humanity.

The trouble is, our novelists and dramatists do

not mean by the denunciation of evil what is meant in other countries. There are two ways of moralizing. One may either inveigh against vice and trace a seductive portrait of virtue, as the preacher does; or depict vice in its repulsive ugliness and leave the reader to draw the moral for himself, as the artist does. It is the second manner which we prefer. We hold that in the bare spectacle of human deformity there is a power of conviction infinitely greater than any that can be generated by the most eloquent exhortations. Let me quote the Abbé Prévost to you once more. In the preface to *Manon Lescaut* he said: "All the precepts of morality are but vague general principles. It is very hard to apply them to actual manners and actions. . . . Only experience or example can reasonably determine the leanings of the heart. Now, experience is not an advantage which it is expedient for everyone to have; it depends on the different situations in which one finds oneself placed by chance. There only remain, then, examples that may serve the rest of us as a guide to conduct in our practice of virtue. It is precisely to this sort of reader that works such as the present may be of extreme utility. . . . Every fact added to it is a ray of light, a precept which supplements experience; every adventure is a model after which one can mould oneself." Lesage, too, expressed himself thus, in speaking of *Guzman*. "All the novels of this sort, although they have little savor or gayety, commonly meet with general approbation. Why? Because their details are pictures of everyday life—portraits which have a corrective quality unperceived by the reader, in that they offer to his eyes presentments which, as they pass through his consciousness, make more impression than all the moral precepts in the world could do. In a word, they instruct by example; and so to instruct, as Mme. Dacier charmingly said, is the distilled essence of philosophy."[3] Paul Bourget made his Claude Larcher express the same idea: "To render visible, almost palpable, the suffering of transgression, the infinite bitterness of evil, the rancor of vice, is to have done a moralist's work; and that is why the melancholy of the *Fleurs du Mal* and of *Adolphe,* the cruelty of the ending of the *Liaisons,* and the sinister atmosphere of *Cousine Bette* make these books achievements of the highest morality."[4]

There follow two important consequences from this fact. First of all, our writers fell into the way of choosing subjects which involve the portrayal of vice, and little by little renounced those which, because they merely place virtue in an attractive light, offer fewer opportunities to awaken the readers' conscience. Then they tended to make their pictures blacker and blacker. If you are going to teach by example, the example must be striking; otherwise it is in danger of passing unnoticed and therefore of missing its object. You have to make evil odious by exaggerating it. To do this is entirely conformable with one of our habits of mind, our preference for generalization. When Molière imagined his Avare he did not see him in the likeness of a particular miser: he combined in his personality traits which he had observed in the various misers encountered during the course of his life, and these traits, combined in a single being, produced an archtype—a synthesis of all the individual examples offered by nature. Harpagon, however true to life in each of his component elements, is nevertheless of a truth so intense that he tends to exaggeration. The same procedure was adopted by most of our great writers. Voltaire claimed this right of amplification. "One must," he said, "paint characters on an elevated plane; there must be no mediocre vices or virtues; a half-tyrant is unworthy of consideration. It is an art to embellish vices and to give them an air of nobility." And Balzac once said to George Sand, in conversing with her at Nohant: "I like exceptional beings. . . . Besides, they are needed to make the common ones stand out, and I never dispense with them unless I have to. But the vulgar interest me more than they do you. Contrary to the procedure of most writers, I ennoble them in their very ugliness and stupidity. I give their deformity terrifying or monstrous proportions. You would not know how to do this; you do well to be blind to creatures and things that would give you nightmares. Idealize the pretty and the beautiful; that is the work for a woman."[5]

To idealize ugliness! That has, in fact, been the formula of our literature, and more especially of our modern literature. You understand now why it is a mistake to infer from the subjects treated by our novelists and dramatists that the nation in general is immoral. Precisely because they have specialized in vice, our writers have neglected a whole section of French society—the most important section of all—which, being well entrenched in its virtuous stability, gave their moralistic tendencies no opportunity. In short, they have depicted only a small minority—one which, to be sure, exists, but which is of too little importance to be taken as representative of our general manners. And even this minority is not depicted in strict accord with the truth, for the magnifying glass is deliberately used in such a way as to accomplish a well-nigh monstrous distortion.

If you want to get a just idea of French morality, it is not, then, to the warped pictures given in our novels and plays that you must look. To know us, you must watch our acts, search out our shortcomings, note our good points; you must not be contented with chance meetings, but must base your opinions on carefully gathered and digested facts; above all, you must be wary of hasty generalizations founded on some isolated incident or on intercourse exclusively with some restricted class whose ways are not those of the whole nation.

You might, to begin with, consult the statistics covering certain aspects of French life. Strictly speaking, it will not be possible to determine exactly the degree of morality attained by each nation until a minute and precise map is drawn to show the distribution of vice and virtue in this world—a sizeable and complicated task, not likely to be accomplished in a moment. But the information which we possess to-day, however incomplete, at least enables us to see clear answers to questions with which we could formerly get nowhere. This information is often very surprising; it overthrows many well-established opinions. Consider, for example, what the statistics reveal about our falling birth rate— one of the arguments most commonly advanced as a proof of French degeneracy. Now, the studies made up to the present time demonstrate that a decreasing natality is by no means confined to France:

it is found everywhere in Europe. And do you know in which of the nations the birth rate is most rapidly diminishing? Germany and England. In 1876-1880 the birth rate in these two countries was respectively 3.92 and 3.54 per hundred inhabitants. In 1913 it was 2.74 and 2.41—that is to say, a diminution of 1.18 per cent for Germany and 1.14 per cent for England. During the same time the birth rate in France had passed from 2.53 to 1.88—a difference of only 0.65 per cent. At the same rate, the percentage of births will be about equal in the three countries in thirty years.[6]

Very interesting, too, are the statistics for illegitimate children. Illegitimacy is not, I know, an absolutely precise indication of the morality of a country; but we shall have to admit that it is one of the least misleading among the signs of laxity of manners. Now, for the year 1910 the European countries which yielded the most favorable percentages were: Holland, 2 per cent; Ireland, 2.8 per cent; Italy and England, 4.1 per cent. Then came Belgium, 6.1 per cent; Scotland, 7 per cent; and France 8.6 per cent. Germany had more than 9 per cent. Japan, Hungary, Denmark, Portugal, Austria, and Roumania had even higher figures. Sweden reached 14.8 per cent.[7] And if we calculate the ratio of the illegitimate births to the number of unmarried women or widows—a method which, according to some statisticians, gives more significant results—the comparison is even more favorable to France. From 1896 to 1905, to every thousand unmarried women or widows the illegitimate births were as follows: Ireland, 3; England and Wales, 8; Scotland, 13; Belgium, 17; France, 18; Denmark, 23; Germany, 26.[8] You can see that, in this list of the nations which do not observe the divine law in the matter of marriage, France is far from occupying a low place. And it should further be remarked that our system of registration of births is so meticulous that not a single illegitimate child can escape the census. One could not say as much of many nations in which the state regulations are so lax that they facilitate all sorts of dissimulations.

The testimony of the figures, then, shows that matters are no worse with us than elsewhere. We actually gain the right to take a severe admonitory attitude toward certain nations which are among those most willing to cast stones at us. Assuredly we are not perfect; our society has its scum. But the soul of the nation is healthy, and its heart is in the right place.

If you want to ascertain as much for yourselves, I advise you to mingle with really French circles. Turn your back on that cosmopolitan group which forms one of the small sections of Parisian society. Try to gain an entry into some worthy family, of no matter what class, in no matter what part of the country. Live the life of that family. You will then have a true idea of the purity and uprightness of French customs.

It is not always easy, to be sure, for you to gain an entry into this sanctuary of our affections. We, who are so affable in society, become almost shy at the prospect of a greater intimacy. The French *foyer* is infinitely more exclusive than the English or American "home." The door is flung wide to relatives, to tried friends. But it is opened only with caution to the knock of strangers; for we feel that the normal play of our existence depends upon its integrity. As long as there has been a France the family has been considered as the foundation of our society. Whereas in the Anglo-Saxon families the nation is the sum of all the individuals of which it is composed, each individual guarding jealously his independence and his rights, in France the true cell of the social organism exists only in that embryo of society formed by the father, the mother, and the children, each of the members surrendering as much of his liberty as is necessary to the solidarity of the group. On this idea of the family all our acts, thoughts, and customs are focused. The founding of a family is the dominant idea of the youth at the period of his development when the delights of sense begin to command his attention; and so it is of the young girl when she awakens to an understanding of the part which she is to play in life. This ruling impulse is what explains our conception of marriage. If love is strongly colored by reason, that is because we hold marriage to be the gravest act of a whole life. When, to this end, two become one, they perceive that their vows exert a binding force likewise on all those who, coming after them, are presently to make the same decision. "We do not marry to please ourselves, whatever may be said to the contrary; we marry quite as much, or more, for the sake of our posterity, our family; custom and the interest served by marriage affect our race long after we are gone," said Montaigne.[9] And the law has sanctioned this principle, in its applications, by surrounding the family with all manner of protective barriers. To insure sound government of the family, the law based its existence on the concept of paternal authority; to enable the family to perpetuate itself, the law gave it the corner-stone of property and put checks on the right to dispose of property by will; to prevent the dislocation of the family by the parents' death where there are minor children, the law substitutes for the natural head of the family a family council empowered to administer the fortune until the majority of the heirs; and to assure the stability of the family, this same law decreed, in bygone days, the indissolubility of marriage.

In this atmosphere of cohesion, the spirit of solidarity is natural and inevitable. Just as juridic community has always constituted our national tradition and our originality in the province of law,[10] so community of sentiment has made the French family an indivisible whole, the stability of which neither adversity nor passion has contrived to shake. In this association, the love of the married pair forms the principal element. For, I dare assert, affection between husband and wife is as frequent in France as it is anywhere else. Nor do I hesitate to maintain that love is fostered more than it is impeded by the fact that the marriage was surrounded with precautions. It has all the more chance to last because disparities of taste, inequalities of position or education—things which are at the root of so much discord—have been eliminated. The ardors of youth last only a brief while; one day or another we must needs settle down to a more placid kind of affection, made up of confidence and mutual concessions. French couples probably attain this state of conjugal sympathy and friendship the more easily because they did not originally base their happiness on the mere summons of desire.

To my thinking, there is nothing in the world more nobly steadfast than one of those typical unions characterized by complete understanding, in which all the relationships of the married pair are controlled by affection—an affection without transports, perhaps, but nevertheless deep. The French husband—all opinions to the contrary notwithstanding—knows no greater pleasure when his day's work is done than to be with his family. The typical French business man would rather close his office for two hours, if necessary, or submit to great physical inconvenience, than miss going home at noon to have luncheon with his family. And the Frenchwoman, correspondingly, knows no greater joy than to watch jealously over the *foyer*. Moreover, she is the sovereign of her *foyer*—a queen before whom everybody bows. If the law has established the priority of the husband, the wife has quietly taken a compensation. You have seen the rôle which she plays in the *salons,* where she rules without a rival and queens it as she will. When the guests have departed, her supremacy remains undisturbed. She is always—to use a locution perfectly expressive of the way we understand her rôle—"the mistress of the house." As early as the seventeenth century the Italian ambassador Lippomano remarked, in speaking of our country: "The married women have more freedom and authority than elsewhere. The husbands entrust the management of the household to them, and even allow themselves to be governed by them." So is it still. French husbands voluntarily abdicate the power which the law has given them. They love to receive support and advice from their wives; they expect them to share their cares, to sustain them in the struggle, to encourage them in their enterprises. How many writers have warmed their talents at the hearts of feminine tenderness! It has often occurred to me that the finest homage which a man could render woman would be to write a history of her influence on French literature. And in all the professions it is the same. Very rare is the Frenchman who has any secrets from her whom the man of the people calls his *"moitié,"* his "better half"—still another expression significant of the equality which we seek in marriage.

From the highest class to the lowest, you will find this same community of thought, this warm and intimate comradeship, this affectionate everyday understanding. And, lest you suspect me of invention—or of self-delusion—I am going to give you examples. Here are two pictures: I borrow them, not from novels, but from memoirs. Both are authentic documents, and there is nothing literary about them except their stylistic charm. The first describes the home surroundings of Ernest Legouvé. Note that he was a dramatist and that his profession compelled him to live among artists—a life supposed to be full of temptations. That did not prevent him from making the best of husbands, as you shall see. In his *Souvenirs* he gives an account of a New Year's vacation during which he was working on a play with his friend Goubaux. This is how his days were spent:

"At seven o'clock in the morning, both of us used to go to my study, in which we would find the fire lighted, the tea served, and the mistress of the house playing for us the part of Lolotte in *Werther,* cutting us slices of bread and butter. A quarter of an hour of hearty laughter, friendly chat; then to work. Seated at the same table, across from one another, we looked like two schoolboys writing compositions. . . . At noon all three of us used to go to luncheon together. I should say all four of us; for my daughter, who was about two years old, made her appearance at that hour, and her astonished eyes, her round pink cheeks, her dress (a triumph of maternal love and coquetry), her gravity as she sat in her little high-chair, the quaintness of her answers (children's ideas are so unexpected that all of them seem to be witty), were one of the pleasures of luncheon. To speak of our work was absolutely forbidden. But that did not prevent my wife from remarking banteringly on the worried or triumphant appearance of each of us, or from deducing gloomy or cheerful prognostications from it. After luncheon, an hour's music, which served for rest, reward, and help. . . . After ten days, Goubaux's vacation being at an end, and our two first acts also, we convened the reading committee. This committee was composed of my wife: 'I am playing the part of Laforêt,' she said as she seated herself in her armchair with her tapestry. Each of us brought his own work, and she added gaily, 'Student Goubaux, I will listen to you first.'

"The double reading led to numerous interruptions. Sometimes I exclaimed as I listened to Goubaux: 'Splendid! It's much better than mine!' 'Don't influence justice,' said my wife. And Justice, having listened to me in my turn and been questioned about her preference between the two acts, answered: 'I think I prefer both of them! Both of them amused me, but not in the same places. I thought M. Goubaux' beginning was much the more striking, but I like the end of the act much better in M. Legouvé's. I like the wife's part best in one and the father's part in the other. . . . It seems to me that a combination of these two versions into one would be a perfect marriage—like ours!' "[11]

Now, another household, also of Paris—that of François Coppée's father. He held a small post at the ministry of war. He had married a penniless young girl, who gave him seven children. The one of them who was later to sing so tenderly of the poor and lowly has described for us in moving words the surroundings in which he grew up:

"The pessimist La Rochefoucauld is wrong when he says bitterly: 'Good marriages there are, but none that are delightful.' I have known one, at any rate, and I should search in vain for another adjective to describe my father's and my mother's life. How they loved one another! And how they loved their children! For them, the problem of making a living was hard indeed. Just think—four children to bring up! My father's modest salary would never have been enough. So my mother, whose handwriting was very good, used to copy out accounts for building contractors, and my two elder sisters, both of whom had some talent for painting, occasionally—very occasionally—sold a copy of a Louvre picture or painted a portrait. Even with so many efforts and so much good will, circumstances were very straitened. . . . Well, in spite of everything those first years of my life have not left me the impression of sadness and poverty. All I remember is the tenderness of all for each and of each for all that reigned in the family. The house was gay. . . . What spread a mysterious charm over this poor dwelling was, I am convinced, the deep and pure love which my father and mother felt for each other.

"I despair of finding words for the impression of unbounded confidence, absolute affection, tender and faithful devotion that was contained in a single look, a single word, that passed between them. According to a habit of the less pretentious parts of society—a habit which I, for one, think admirable—they used *tu* in addressing each other. My mother called her husband 'Coppée.' He, in turn, sometimes called his wife by her pet name, Rose; at other times he would say, *'maman.'* At such times he seemed to think of himself as one of the children—and he was not far wrong, gentle simple-hearted dreamer that he was. In my mother's attitude toward this man, so good, so simple, so much at the mercy of life's dangers, there was indeed a touch of the maternal. I do not mean that this admirable woman, so intelligent and hardworking, so brave and gay even in the darkest days, ruled the household or, in the racy phrase of the common people, "portât les culottes"—wore the breeches; on the contrary, she contrived that the authority of the head of the household and the respect which were due him never seemed to be endangered in the eyes of his children; and though he was the most indulgent and mild-tempered of men, our mother's invariable formula when we committed some little fault was: 'What would your father say? If your father knew, it would make him so unhappy!'

"Let me reconstruct from memory a few hours

of my early childhood in this family, unblessed with worldly goods, yet so united, honest, and respectable.

"It is a summer evening. The dining-room window is open, and one can hear the twittering of birds in the neighboring park. The older sisters, Annette and Sophie, one fair and one dark, both pretty, dressed very simply but with taste—for they are Parisiennes—have just come back from the Musée, carrying their paint-boxes, and laid the table. When, presently, the father comes in, bringing a cake for dessert—for it is pay-day, or, as he laughingly says, Sainte-Touche—all there is left to do is to sit down to table. Father installs himself in his straw-bottomed armchair. . . . The two young women take their places on either side of him, and to the left of mother's still empty place (she is busy in the kitchen), he sees his third daughter, nine years old—the one they call 'fat Marie' because of her round cheeks and her sturdy appearance—and finally his son, five years old, the only male and the inheritor of the name, raised up on his chair by six volumes of the *Magasin Pittoresque!* What a happy smile on the good man's face! And, when the mistress of the house appears at last, carrying the smoking soup-tureen in both hands, with what a joyful voice he greets her! 'We're dying of hunger—sit down quickly, *maman*, and help us to soup.' Ah! that family dinner table! those frugal dinners of long ago, at which our dear and delightful father, to enliven the young people clustered around him, was wont to talk with so much wit and sparkle, and, following the precept of Mme. Scarron, often to replace the roast by a story! Dinner over, we would pass into the next room (where the conjugal couch was hidden in an alcove behind a curtain), and the evening would begin. In the big trees, the tops of which we could see through the windows, the birds were silent, and the first stars were already coming out. Then our busy mother would light the lamp, settle herself at her little table, and, in no wise distracted by the duet which her two big daughters were playing at the old square piano, resume copying in her fine legible hand (which I have inherited from her) some memorandum about joinery or locksmith's work. As for the two children—that is to say, my sister Marie and me—they were already seated on stools at their father's feet, knowing very well that after the music there would be stories."[12]

In these two pictures, representative of two very different households, you have doubtless noticed points of resemblance which show them to be akin. The fact is, they contain the most characteristic traits of the real French family: the domesticity of the husband, his disposition to put himself under the protection of his wife; her tender devotion, her industry, her attention to even the most humble details of the household, and above all the part she plays as moral or intellectual adviser. And now perhaps you understand the delight experienced by Barrett Wendell when, to his great surprise, he discovered this type of the true Frenchwoman: "In all human language, I believe, there was never gathered together more admirable significance than you shall find, when you come emotionally to understand them, in the French words *honnête femme*. The Frenchwomen who deserve to be so called are countless everywhere throughout France. They are not only the most admirable type of French womanhood; they are the most pervasive, the most frequent, the most profoundly characteristic. That they are not always the most instantly evident to careless, to foreign, to artistic eyes is partly because, like light and air, you shall find them wherever you go; and partly because their unrepining devotion to their absorbing duties keeps them inconspicuous. They would not be themselves if they were not conjugally faithful—and faithful not only in personal constancy, the sense most instantly implied by these terms, but faithful also in devotion to their husbands throughout the complicated and perplexing cares of incessant responsibility; conjugal love would not be enough without life-long conjugal friendship too. But all the conjugal love and friendship imaginable would not suffice, either, without faithful observance of domestic duties as well, in all their intricate range.'"[13]

It should be added that this union between married people is all the closer for being accompanied by another sentiment, one almost stronger than conjugal love: love of the children. There are countries in which to found a family means to unite for good or for evil the existence of two beings who are convinced that they were made for one another. In France, to found a family is that, indeed; but also, and above all, it is to continue the chain whose links were forged by our ancestors—to perpetuate that store of memories and interest, unspeakably precious in our eyes, which has been handed down to us, and of which we are the temporary custodians. Therefore children, as soon as they appear in the home, are not only the objects of their parents' tenderness, but actually the end which the whole existence of those parents is to serve thenceforth. To them, because they are the hope of the future, are sacrificed comfort, liberty—everything. To insure their happiness is a constant care.

This preoccupation becomes so absorbing that it amounts almost to a tyranny. The child, so long as he belongs to the family group, remains the property of his parents, and they make all the important decisions about his future, his education, the choice of his career; even about the choice of the one in conjunction with whom he in his turn is to found a family.

You reproach us, I am aware, with this firm hold of ours on the hearts and minds of our children. You say that the domination exercised by French parents kills all initiative and spirit of adventure in the young people; that free development of the individual is hampered and often curtailed. And that is certainly true. But that is precisely what we are trying to accomplish. I cannot insist too strongly on this point. The family is not, with us, simply the common life of individuals held together by affection and at the same time preserving their independence: it is an organism whose every part is united with the utmost solidarity to every other part—such a solidarity as is impossible without a complete sacrifice of each member's happiness to that of every other member. This renunciation of personal liberty—and it is made by the parents quite as unconditionally as by the children—is the indispensable condition of unity in the French family. The love of each individual is impregnated with consciousness of sacrifice

MORALS AND FAMILY LIFE

made for a higher aim than personal gratification or the mere pursuit of pleasure.

You now see why, in this chapter on morals, I have been led quite naturally into talking to you of the French family. The French family is at once the source of our duties and the school in which we practice them. It teaches the children to respect authority, to obey, and to love order; to the parents it teaches devotion, renunciation, and unselfishness; to all it demonstrates the advantage of solidarity and the necessity of each member's helping to bear the sorrows of those dear to him. There are no individual or social virtues which are not developed in family life as we understand it. And so we can say in conclusion: "Blessed be France, for she has kept alive the cult of the family!" So long as she jealously preserves this cult there can be no misgivings on the score of morality; for she will experience no loosening of social bonds, no triumph of mere brute instinct or defeat of noble and lofty sentiments.

VIII

Politics and Religion

NO doubt you are surprised to have me join in the same title two matters so different as the conduct of political affairs and the soul's well-being. In America such an association would be impossible. Your churches hold themselves aloof from the various ins and outs of government and confine themselves to moral principles. If at times they arm for the fray, it is in connection with partisan struggles which do not interfere with their legitimate religious aspirations. They live on good terms with the different governmental parties. And your administrations, in turn, know the church only as an organization subject to the common law, in whose affairs they do not dream of meddling. Church and state form two distinct worlds, with clearly differentiated interests.

In France, on the contrary, church and state are inextricably interwoven. I do not see how I could speak of one without touching on the history of the other. The church exercises a constant influence on the status of the political parties, and is perforce either an ally or an enemy. The state, in consequence, is obliged to have a religious policy—a policy so determinate that it may sometimes become of prime importance, and even affect all parliamentary strategy.

In the few years before 1914 the relations between church and state reached the stage of open war. Perceiving this, certain historians (foreigners for the most part), taking into account only the momentary state of things, imagined that they had deciphered the reason for the antagonism in some inherent tendencies of the French mind. The Frenchman, they say, is foredoomed to atheism by his belief in reason. He it was who inaugurated that philosophical movement of the eighteenth century which logically ended in the war against religion. The conflict between church and state which took place in France throughout the nineteenth century was, then, inevitable.

Such reasoning is false. France is not the only country which has known religious dissensions. The England of the sixteenth century did away with Roman Catholicism in a somewhat brutal manner. The Italy of Cavour persecuted the religious communities and appropriated their possessions without scruple. Germany had the Kulturkampf, the tyrannical violence of which far exceeded the timid attacks of the French state against the church. Our leaning toward rationalism, therefore, cannot be the only factor in the case. More complex and far more remote are the causes of the inextricable confusion of political aims and religious aspirations in France. It is in the tangled web of our long history that we must search for these causes.

It is not too much to say that modern France owes to the church its political unity, and perhaps its very existence politically. (By the church I mean the Catholic church, and in the whole of this chapter that is the meaning which I shall invariably give to the word; the Protestant and Jewish communities are not numerically important in France.) When the barbarians invaded Gaul, the Catholic church was the only vigorous organization left in the decaying Roman state. Its firmly established hierarchy gave it an authority which the territorial dissolution ensuing upon the fall of the Western Empire merely consolidated. It exercised a considerable power, gained from slowly accumulated privileges. It was richly endowed. It was invested not only with spiritual jurisdiction, but also with temporal; for it judged the clergy in all causes into which religion entered, and it possessed an arbitral jurisdiction in the litigation which the faithful agreed to submit to it. The bishops had, moreover, inherited from the Empire a certain number of rights which placed them above ordinary magistrates. For example, they acted as overseers to the judges, whose abuses they could denounce; they participated in the nomination of guardians and curators. They belonged, too, to rich families, and by virtue of their education they formed the élite of the country. In their persons the church united not only the prestige which is attached to spiritual supremacy and to learning, but also the influence which always accompanies wealth and birth.[1]

It is therefore not surprising that, in the disorder which succeeded the fall of the Empire and the fury of the invasions, the populace should have gathered around the church as around a protector capable of defending their interests. The bishops, strengthened by this allegiance, had no difficulty in imposing themselves on the Frankish monarchs; their position and their power made them indispensable as intermediaries between the barbarians and the autochthonous inhabitants. Clovis, by his conversion, gave official recognition to an alliance which in point of fact already existed. And from that day the fate of the church was allied to that of the monarchy, the success of one being a sort of guarantee of the other's security. We know how ardently the bishops abetted and even instigated Clovis in all his undertakings. Indeed, "the establishment of the Franks in Gaul was to a very considerable extent the work of the church." It is not without reason that Gregory of Tours gave his history of Clovis the title *Histoire ecclésiastique des Francs,* or that France has always been regarded as the "eldest daughter" of the church.[2]

And so it was with all of Clovis's successors. The Merovingian kings sometimes treated the church brutally; but they let it play a preponderating part in the government of the country. A great number of bishops lived at the palace near the king, whose respected ministers they were. It was to them that royalty appealed for inforcement of the laws or for counsel in important affairs. Those who resided in the dioceses exercised a greater authority than did the counts. Bishops presided over assemblies of priests and laymen, made administrative decisions over the heads of civil representatives, and even took over the government of cities.

With the Carolingian kings the alliance between church and state became still closer. Pépin le Bref, in order to counterbalance the power of the great vassals, had the bishops enter the *Champ de Mars,* not only as landowners, but in their episcopal character; and the bishops "from that time on took a preponderating part in the councils about legislation and administration." Charlemagne continued the policy of his father. It appears that he even dreamed of founding an universal empire of which the church was to have been the unshakable foundation. He considered himself the overlord of his bishops just as truly as of his counts.[3] His easy-going successors went still farther. By consecration the princes had already submitted themselves to the unction of the church—a fact which made their position dependent upon its sanction. In 856 Charles the Bald granted the bishops power to undo what they had done—to dethrone kings who were unworthy. And even when this privilege had to be abandoned, consecration remained the symbol of the union between throne and altar, subscribed to by the first Frankish kings.[4] Thus, by virtue of circumstances integral with the growth of France, the church found itself bound to the civil government and indeed almost indistinguishable from it. And the chain forged by five centuries of history, from the fifth to the tenth, was never broken.

In proportion as the French monarchy grew aware of its strength and felt the growing desire for absolute power, the church did, to be sure, lose its supremacy. Caught up in the feudal organization, its fate coincided with that of the great vassals; it had to submit, as they did, to lay authority. To the theory of the "direct power of the church over the state" which had triumphed during the early centuries, there succeeded the theory of the "direct power of the state over the church."[5] When, in 1516, Francis I signed the first Concordat with the Pope, he made the clergy dependent on the king. And the weight of this dependence became gradually greater, until the culminating triumph of the theory of absolute monarchy under Louis XIV, when the king tried to make himself "head of a national church."

But the union between church and state was no less close for having undergone a change. The two powers had the same interests, and in the hour of danger they gave each other mutual support. When the papacy tried to take away the temporal power of the churches or arrogated to itself the right to dispose of ecclesiastical benefices, our kings took up the defense of their church. Likewise, the clergy of France upheld the king whenever the papacy encroached on the royal prerogatives. Thus, when Gregory XIV declared Henry IV to be deprived of all his rights and by two monitory bulls threatened the clergy, the nobility, and the people with excommunication if they did not abandon their king, an assembly of cardinals, bishops, abbots, and others, held at Chartres, declared that "the said monitions, interdictions, suspensions, and excommunications are null and void, both in form and matter; that they are unjust and instigated by the artifices of foreigners who are enemies of France; and that they cannot bind or oblige French Catholics who are obedient to the King" (September 21, 1591).[6]

In recompense for its submission and its services the church received privileges and, what was more, a great deal of special consideration. Loyseau wrote in the seventeenth century: "But in this very Christian kingdom, we have kept the most honorable place for the Ministers of God, rightly making of the Clergy—that is to say, of the Ecclesiastical order—the first of the three Estates of France. . . . Herein we have followed the ancient Gauls, our predecessors, who gave the first place to the Druids, who were their Priests, and whom they even chose as Judges and Magistrates.'" Article 45 of an edict of April, 1695, registered on May 14, confirms this tradition, which Loyseau, as you have seen, traced back to the very origin of our country: "We desire the archbishops," it said, "the bishops, and all other ecclesiastics to be honored as the first of the orders of our kingdom and that they should be upheld in all the rights, honors, ranks, precedences, and jurisdictions which they have enjoyed or should have enjoyed up to the present time." And in the Estates General the deputies of the clergy took rank immediately after the princes of the blood royal, and before the nobility. In all the assemblies of their diocese the archbishops and bishops had precedence over the governors.[8] If, in the course of centuries, the prestige of the church was sometimes dimmed, it was never for long. Under the old régime the church was always a power on which our kings loved to lean, which they unfailingly honored, and to which they were sometimes forced to bow.

You understand now why the clergy of France, from having been so long associated with the government of the country, came to consider themselves as an integral part of the state. They regarded the right of the priest to deal with temporal matters, regulating them for the benefit of spiritual interests, as natural, imprescriptible, and salutary to the nation. And until the end of the eighteenth century nobody contested this right. The Revolution struck the first serious blow against an idea which had come to be as deeply rooted in the minds of laymen as of the clergy. In the eyes of the revolutionary party, the privileged church appeared no whit less odious than the nobility itself. One of the first concerns of the Constituent Assembly was to abolish its privileges, confiscate its revenues (such as tithes and surplice fees), and declare all ecclesiastical possessions to be the property of the nation. To do this was to take from the church one of the most considerable sources of its power; and the clergy of the time would have given proof of a superhuman disinterestedness had they accepted without protest the overthrow of an order established for more than thirteen centuries. From that day the church of France found itself in the paradoxical situation of having to oppose every democratic movement as if it were inherently antagonistic to religion. Established in order to watch over the spiritual well-being of all, it was condemned in self-defense to oppose the majority of the faithful.

The struggle between church and state, however, did not reach a serious crisis until the Third Republic. After some years, during which it was put to terrible proof, the church regained from the Concordat of 1801 a part of its importance; it was officially recognized as one of the great powers of the state. And if Napoleon tried to make of it merely an instrument for consolidating his own power; even if, as Montholon wittily said, it was reduced to "a holy police-force"—at least, to belong to the police was to be on the side of power! Under the Restoration and the Second Empire, the church might even have dreamed that she had regained all her former influence. It was only after the Franco-Prussian war of 1870, when the republic was established, that the antagonism of the public powers burst out. The church, remembering revolutionary times and warned by the anti-clerical measures of 1830 and 1848, saw, not without apprehension, the growing influence of the popular party. It is certain that the clergy hoped for the overthrow of the new government and gave its support to the royalist groups in their efforts to reëstablish the monarchy. The republicans rose at once against this avowed enemy, and their antagonism burst into open flame on the day when, in May, 1877, Gambetta pronounced the famous phrase: "Clericalism—that is the enemy!" Hostility between the partisans and the enemies of the Catholic church only increased from that time on, to attain its supreme intensity about 1880, when Jules Ferry, following the path marked out by Germany, introduced into France a sort of Kulturkampf. From that moment our whole national life has been dominated by religious struggles; and for more than thirty years the political parties, whatever their programmes or objectives, have grouped themselves into two opposing camps, the clerical and the anti-clerical.

The details of the struggle between these two groups are no doubt present in your minds, and I will not recall them. I will limit myself to singling out one episode, that which constituted the crisis of this drama—the Dreyfus affair and its consequence, the separation of church and state. I mention it here because it has seemed to me that the significance and the far-reaching consequence of this incident were not well understood abroad. I recognize that it is very difficult for anyone but a Frenchman to grasp the remote causes of the affair.

Neither politics nor religion was palpably involved: what was involved was simply a decision made by a court of justice. An officer had been condemned as a traitor: had he been wrongfully condemned? That was the problem. But it was found that the man in question was a Jew; and the Jews could not be exonerated from the charge of having incited the republic to make war on Catholicism. It was also found that the officers who had condemned Captain Dreyfus were, by birth and conviction, fervent Catholics. To the aid of the accused flocked all the enemies of the church, and round the accusers rallied all the defenders of the church. Thus the struggle was carried into the province of clericalism and anti-clericalism. The adversaries of twenty years found themselves face to face; and once more they persuaded themselves that the victory of one of the two parties would mean the disappearance of the other from French politics.

The anti-clericals, Dreyfusards for the most part, were in power. They had strength behind them, and they could not resist the temptation to use it. Rightly or wrongly, they felt themselves obliged to crush once for all an organization which endangered their existence. They did not choose the wisest or the cleverest means, perhaps. They decided to break the bonds that still attached the church to the state; they undertook the revocation of the Concordat of 1801.

It must be admitted that, in the negotiations and discussions which took place, faults were committed on both sides. Neither our political men nor the Vatican treated the question with ideal dispassionateness. At Rome a Spanish priest was leading pontifical politics. He had no sympathy for France, and he preached a haughty and uncompromising resistance. As in the best days of our history, the French clergy showed themselves, from motives of patriotism, ready for certain compromises. They accepted the *associations cultuelles* or councils which were charged with the administration of the churches under the control of the state. The Vatican opposed its veto. The French government softened the measure by leaving to the priests and the faithful the control of the churches, under a simple form of declaration. The Vatican opposed its veto. On the other side, the French politicians were too often blinded by passion and gave proof of an extraordinary narrowness of mind. Anti-clericalism constituted the whole programme of some of them. These urged an extreme course; and one of the most extraordinary spectacles of the time was to see the very government which was resolutely working for separation obliged to check the impatience of its partisans and recommend concessions and tolerance.

The separation of church from state was proclaimed. But the effects of the decision were considerably weakened when the government consented to leave to the clergy the free disposition of the churches and the personal property necessary to the practice of worship. Only the stipends were done away with, the priests henceforth being forced to count on the generosity of the congregation. In fact, a state of affairs was instituted quite comparable to that obtaining in America. Church and state were completely independent of each other.

For the government it was as much a defeat as a victory; for the state had had to abandon the control over the church which it so desired to keep. All things considered, I am tempted to say that it was more a defeat than a victory. For the church, in ceasing to be official, acquired an independence which it had never had. The bishops, no longer chosen by the government, the priests, no longer functionaries, could henceforth use all their influence with impunity in the service of parties hostile to the Republic. The entire clergy was now to receive its inspiration from Rome without the counterbalancing influence of national interests. People had got rid of a "state within a state," which was a mere phrase; and they had given up a control which was an actual fact. Delivered from a jealous guardian, the church emerged formidable from the trial—all the more formidable because the Frenchman is chivalrous by nature and given to taking the part of the defeated. After the separation the number of the faithful in the churches increased. It became good form to be Catholic, and people became most aggressively Catholic. The denunciation of the Concordat contributed in no slight degree to the religious revival which was noticeable shortly before the war. In 1914 the church stood out against the state, more powerful than ever; and more than ever, it seemed, our politics were going to be dominated by the struggle between clericalism and anti-clericalism.

The extreme importance which we have accorded religion in our political parties has had its inconveniences. The various successive administrations have, to be sure, accomplished solid work. Betterment of the poor, relief committees and provident associations, laws of hygiene, development of education—such have been the preoccupations of our statesmen. All in all, I think there are few countries in which the legislative body has done its work with more zeal—a zeal which has seemed to some almost excessive. But, as soon as one has done justice to the work accomplished, one must admit that political discussions of a theoretical sort have taken far too large a place in our national life. Intellectual energy which should have been used for the study of urgent reforms has often been exhausted by interminable controversies. Religious quarrels have too often displaced the axis of French politics by mingling spiritual preoccupations with purely worldly interests. The struggle for the domination of a particular party has never been a creative effort; but when a nation goes to the length of subordinating the rational administration of a country to debates on questions of faith—that is to say, on what pertains to beliefs held in the most secret recesses of the mind—then one is entitled to suspect those who are so engaged of having lost all sense of reality.

And it is precisely because our quarrels were outside the realm of practical reality that they were so bitter. It was a question not of individuals, not even of the preëminence of a party, but simply of the triumph of an idea. Those who thought they detected in these antagonisms the signs of rivalry or ambition little knew the French mind. If the French were filled with such combative zeal, it was because they found in their adversaries a conception of human life contrary to the belief which they themselves professed, a belief which they held to be irrefutable. Even those who least rationalized their views felt that, in this struggle, two ideal concepts were in conflict. The partisans of Catholicism saw with terror the principle of authority endangered. To them the church represented an organization as firm as it was old, to which must be granted the honor of having established our society on an unshakable basis, and which had retained enough of its strength to yoke together the conflicting forces generated by the conditions of modern life. To its enemies the church appeared to be the most powerful obstacle to progress —that progress which they dated from the Revolution, and which they wanted to bring to a complete development in a world in which, all men being equal, there were to be no classes or ranks. Those who saw farther and were capable of putting their ideas into philosophical terms discovered profounder causes underneath this antagonism between liberty and authority. In the struggle they recognized the opposition of two irreconcilable philosophical concepts. On the one hand was the belief that life proceeds according to the laws of evolution and that it is anti-scientific to try to ignore those laws. France is the logical product of a long past, during the course of which society has been transformed slowly and naturally, like any living organism. We are jointly and severally the outcome of this past, just as the future will be the outcome of the present. It would be folly to try to thwart the meaning of these transformations; it would be especially dangerous to tamper with the church, which has been intimately bound up with our history, and which, indeed, has moulded that history. On the other hand we have the alternative belief: the past is the past —we must think only of the future. Evolutionary developments are too slow for the taste of the masses, hungry for their share of the good things of the world. If the past failed to procure universal happiness, then so much the worse for the past; the only thing to do is to break with it entirely. Let us substitute revolution for evolution. In 1789 a few days sufficed to abolish privileges and to make everybody equal. Let us be as bold as our fathers. Every old institution, and first and foremost the church, must be pitilessly destroyed if it is an obstacle to the rapid overthrow of a hated order and to the establishment of the society of the future.

To sum up: on one side we have history, tradition, evolution, and authority; on the other, philosophy, experiment, revolution, and liberty. And, indeed, these were the very words which echoed more or less clearly in the minds of the French people, sounding like calls to arms and showing, too, how deeply the quarrel had become lost in the maze of abstractions and absolute ideas. Now, as you will remember, the Frenchman is very prone to go to extremes when ideas are in question. If material interests had been at stake, his innate common sense would infallibly have found a medium course—some compromise acceptable to both parties. But the moment principles were involved, any admission that there could be a particle of truth in the opposing conception became an insult to good faith, an infidelity to truth. "Truth is truth, and there is only one truth." These words— one of our most persistent dogmas—did duty as a motto in our religious controversies. People rushed madly into the battle to fight for the triumph of truth, just as they had so often done in the course of our history, and just as they would do to-morrow if a new occasion or a new event brought some essential principle into discussion. And in the high altitudes at which politics was kept, the parties felt a sort of purification. For they acted in good faith, they thought they were fighting for an ideal, for the good of the country; and to this ideal, to this good, they were ready to sacrifice everything.

But, precisely because the dispute was abstract, the conflict was more violent in appearance than in fact. A peculiarity of contests of ideas is that they take place in a sort of unreal world and therefore escape the influence of the passions, properly so called. The adversaries in such cases are like lawyers who abuse each other and almost come to blows in the courtroom, but who are the best of friends again directly they have taken off their gowns in the vestibule. If you have been present at a meeting of the Chambre des Députés—if you have even read our papers regularly—you must have had the impression that France was divided into two irreconcilable camps, the adherents of which were ready to cut each other's throats. In reality, clericals and anti-clericals, as soon as they leave the irritating atmosphere of politics, live very happily together. The priests go about their business quietly, and I have never seen the fiercest anti-clerical speak to an ecclesiastic otherwise than politely, and often (so strong a force is habit) deferentially. Friendships, even, are common between clericals and anti-clericals —certainly a proof of the adage that opposites attract each other! I know a university professor who at the elections would not vote for a candidate with the slightest leaning toward Catholicism, but who nevertheless is on the best of terms with all the priests of the town. Among the students he seems to prefer the ecclesiastics; and these cannot speak loudly enough in his praise.

The fact is that, in spite of the conflicting principles for which men fight, the gulf between adversaries is not so wide as might be supposed. These hostile brothers have raised between themselves a barricade from behind which they hurl threats and insults, and they believe it to be insurmountable. But it is only the thickness of this barrier which separates them; and to do away with it by common accord would be all that is needed to enable the combatants to shake hands. In the bottom of his heart the Frenchman is always religious. We have here one more example of the duality of our nature, the fundamental contradictions which we have repeatedly noticed. In vain does the Latin in us call upon the love of reason and take arms against whatever is not evident to the intelligence: the Celt in us persists in indulging his love of mystery, his insatiable curiosity as to what is beyond this life. Not for nothing was France for centuries the advance guard of the Christian nations. The people who in the Middle Ages caused the most wondrous of the world's churches to spring from the soil, and who took a preëminent part in the crusades, cannot be other than religious. When faith has possessed a country for centuries, it can hardly disappear in a few decades. Those among you who have travelled in France have seen for yourselves that religion is still a very living thing in our country. The churches are as numerous as of yore; they rear their delicately pierced spires as proudly to the sky; the bells still peal out their carillons joyously or sadly, calling the congregation to prayer. In town as well as countryside you can see crowds of believers attending the services which succeed one another throughout the morning of a Sunday. Even in Paris, citadel of the unbelieving, the majority of the population are practicing Catholics and partake of the sacraments. The finger of scorn is pointed at the child who has not been baptized or has not made his first communion. As for the church wedding, people hardly dare dispense with it, and the couple who content themselves with the benediction of the mayor seem to themselves, you may be sure, no more than half married. Before such considerations, political beliefs become of slight importance. It is not at all uncommon to hear a notorious anti-clerical declare one day that the great enemy, clericalism, must be wiped out, and the next day to see him dress himself in his Sunday best to be present at his little daughter's first communion. And it is with tears in his eyes that he follows the adored figure of that child of his. How lovely she seems to him under her white veil, as she steps by with lowered eyes, her whole mind filled with God, in the procession led by the clergy in their vestments! At that moment he forgets his hatred of the priest; and, whether he admits it or no, the old beliefs that have lain slumbering in his heart awaken softly and begin to stir. And on that day when Death comes knocking at the door with imperious hand, how the irreligious notions dissolve and fade in the mist into which we are to pass! Save for a few occasional exceptions—men who have determined to be inexorably logical to the end, the occasional intellectual who has so closely reasoned out his convictions that recantation is no longer possible to him, the politician who is jealous of his posthumous renown—the Frenchman, whatever his political professions may have been during his life, summons the priest for the last consolations.

But, you will say, to practice Catholicism is not the same thing as being truly religious. I agree with you that to go to the services and receive the sacraments is not enough in itself to prove the sincerity, and still less the depth, of religious feeling. But the Frenchman has no tendency to mysticism. Though by no means immune from the shudder which the uncertainty of the Beyond sends through the soul, he rarely falls into despair. He has always tried to keep the flights of his imagination within reasonable limits. In his transports he likes to feel the ground firm underneath his feet. If he admits that he should bow in adoration before the mystery of life, he is also convinced that to love God does not entail the sacrifice of all earthly joys. The Frenchman feels the need of a religion which makes the best of temporal things while respecting the rights of spiritual ones—a religion which shall be rather a link binding mankind together than an invitation to find individual salvation in an austere retirement from the world.

And that is precisely the reason why Catholicism is so deeply rooted in the soul of the Frenchman. This religion has satisfied the most imperious requirements of his mind. It is human, for it founded its dogma of redemption on the axiom that, since man is weak, indulgence must be vouchsafed that weakness. Now, the Frenchman will readily admit that the mind is not free; that it drags after itself the ball-and-chain of the material body. Catholicism is eminently social; for by propagating the doctrine of vicarious goodness—the idea that the worthy may be worthy in behalf of others, to their common benefit (*justi merere possunt pro aliis de congruo*)—it established a vast communism of virtue, a mighty commonwealth of believers. And, you remember, sociability is one of the prime qualities to a Frenchman—one of the most imperious of his needs. There is no instinct of his which Catholicism does not satisfy. Even his centralizing tendency is fulfilled by its model of a hierarchy solidly organized under the person of its one all-powerful head.

When the philosopher, taking these circumstances into account, scans the long perspective of our history, he cannot help being surprised that there should ever have been a struggle between the state and the church in France. Neither does the fact that this struggle particularly characterizes the Republican régime suffice to explain such an inversion of the logic of things. For there is nothing in the Catholic dogma which is opposed to the democratic ideal. Heir to Christianity, Catholicism was proud to be the religion of the humble, and in certain of its principles it is akin to socialism—so nearly akin that we have seen a considerable fraction of the French clergy join the people and put themselves at the people's service in order to further their claims. Are not the French clergy, moreover, almost exclusively recruited from among the sons of peasants? It would take but little to give to both parties the sudden perception that they have been drawn into the battle by an incredible illusion, and that it is possible to reconcile the points at variance by merging them into some more comprehensive idea—for example, the welfare of France.

That such an understanding is possible was shown us by the war. The sacred union (and, by the way, is not this very phrase a revelation of the religious idealism of the French soul?) drew together not merely the different creeds—Catholics, Protestants, Jews, which up to that time had been suspicious of each other—but also the free-thinkers. And it united them in a single sentiment which attained to the fervor of a genuine religion: patriotism. The clergy and the Catholics, forgetting their grievances against the government, saw in that government only the embodiment of France; and they rushed to its aid with no other thought than to save the very entity which for nearly twenty years they had been trying to overthrow. The partisans of the Republican régime, too—even the most extreme of them—greeted their brothers with open arms and collaborated with them in a spirit of fraternal cordiality. You might have seen the secretary of a workmen's union and an archbishop sitting side by side, discussing together in an atmosphere of concord and good-will the means of saving the common mother. The government itself, all false pride relinquished, recognized the moral power of the church and sued for its coöperation. And its coöperation was never refused.

The habit of tolerance is now engendered: there is no obstacle to its persisting. I cannot believe that, at the worst, religious and political disputes will have the same rancor henceforth as in the past. Their futility in the hour of peril has been proved; the same futility persists, though the danger is no more. The union of us all has, moreover, become a necessity if we wish to raise France from its ruins.

Everybody is convinced of this truth. Rare are those who refuse nowadays to see that four years of war and mourning profoundly modified our ways of thinking and feeling. Everyone speaks tolerantly. At the time of the last elections the Catholics promised to forget the past and to cease their attacks against the Republic. The Republicans likewise proclaimed that henceforward other cares must occupy the attention of legislators anxious for the country's welfare, and that exhausting quarrels about principles were no longer relevant when there was so much reconstruction necessary. Only a few days ago[9] M. Millerand, president of the council, was asked by someone whether he intended to resume relations with the Vatican. He replied that he would have only the interests of the nation at heart. It is not difficult to determine the precise meaning hidden under this diplomatic phrase. I think I can safely predict that people are going soon to witness the official reconciliation of church and state in France. That would mean a definite religious equilibrium; and there might be a renewal of the movement inaugurated in 1894 under the name of *l'esprit nouveau*. The policy of general tolerance and mutual support which was the dream of Spüller, and which was approved by Pope Leo XIII—a policy both intelligent and rich in practical possibilities—would then become a reality. The consequences might be incalculable. From such an alliance the two contracting parties could but gain. The church would derive a reassurance of spiritual power; the government, rid of an adversary whom it has never succeeded in defeating and fortified by the great store of moral authority newly placed at its disposal, could at last devote itself unhampered to those difficult tasks which will suffice to fill the years to come. Finally, in the renewed calm, the mind of France would be released from a contradiction which has long bewildered so many brains. The intellectual powers and the hereditary instincts would no longer be in opposition; nay, they would blend as in the finest days of our history. Such a consummation would undoubtedly be a gain to the progress and prestige of French civilization.

IX

The Mission of France

I HAVE hesitated a long time before adopting the title given to this chapter. It is not so long ago that we often heard another people speak with pride of its "historical mission." And we know now what they meant by those words: the instinct of domination, the lust of conquest, the crushing of the weak, the glorification of might. In consequence the word "mission" is used to-day in a somewhat derogatory sense, and it awakens legitimate apprehensions in those who hear it. I shall stick to it, nevertheless, if only to restore its good name. For, as you shall see, this phrase, when applied to France, evokes no memory of which we need feel ashamed. Indeed, it recalls a long history of justice, beauty, altruism, and humaneness. I am going, moreover, to use it in a very exact sense and in order to express an indisputable truth. Every nation in the world has a particular rôle which its qualities and temperament have fitted it to play. We have seen that France has a very distinct individuality; and it is legitimate to ask in what way her national peculiarities have determined her conduct in the world—what, in short, is the place occupied by France in the history of the nations, and what her part in the progress of civilization. Such an attempt is the natural conclusion of this long study of the French mind.

I shall begin with the point on which opinion is

unanimous: the prestige which our artists and authors have always had. This is a subject on which even our enemies have been unstinting in their praise. It was, I believe, Nietzsche who said: "France is the seat of intellectual culture and the most refined school of taste in Europe." And I think I can say without boasting that we clearly merit this eulogy. Our instinct for moderation and dislike of extremes —a quality already described as characteristic of the French mind—makes us choose as if automatically the thing which is harmonious and pleasing. It is incontrovertible that from every French production —be it the composition of a picture, the lines of a public building, the perspective of a garden or street, the folds of a dress, the arrangement of a room, the chasing of a jewel, the gilding of a binding, the form of a tool, or the structure of a steel bridge—there emanates an impression of charm and delicacy, grace and nobility, clarity and calm—in a word, a feeling of distinction; that inclusive quality summed up in the word "*cachet.*" Other nations may have more originality in the invention of forms of art, more fire in the execution; but there are, I think, none who provide the connoisseur with purer, rarer, or more delicate æsthetic delights. I need no other proof than the flattering homage which you Americans have paid us. To a Frenchman visiting your galleries, it is a delightful surprise to observe the preëminent place occupied by our artists. In Boston, Chicago, New York, in private houses— everywhere, the finest collections of our works. There are few picture galleries, even in France, which can offer so numerous and so perfect examples of the Barbizon School or of our impressionists.

Dupré, Rousseau, Daubigny, Corot, Diaz, Jules Breton, Millet, Meissonier, Detaille, Rosa Bonheur, Regnault, Bastien Lepage, Henner, Degas, Monet, Manet, Sisley, Renoir, Gaston Latouche, Pissarro, and many more have found a luxurious and triumphal home in your country. Actually, if you continue to admire our painters with such an acquisitive fervor, in a few years it will be to America that people will have to come if they want to study the French school.

Even deeper has been the penetration of our intellectual life. For more than eight centuries we have been the leaders in the march of ideas. "The whole intellectual development of Latin Europe is French," said Brownell.[1] He might have gone farther and said "the whole intellectual development of Europe"; for in every country of the Old World—in England, Germany, Russia, the Balkans—there is no cultivated man but makes it a point of honor to speak our language and to know our literature. Ever since we have had writers at all, we have never ceased to elaborate and perfect theories, to seek out new systems in order to win progressively nearer to that ultimate truth for which we yearn. The Frenchman may seem timid in the practical affairs of life; but in the boundless land of ideas his audacity knows no obstacles. Accustomed to think freely, chafing under the constraint of ready-made opinions, the deadening influence of a fixed ideal, he throws himself headlong into the discovery of intellectual problems. He meditates, analyzes, dissects; he is never satisfied with the results gained; again and again he demolishes what he has so painfully built up; he exhausts himself with his efforts, his very anxiety urging him to countless new beginnings, bolder and bolder explorations, more and more exact approximations of the absolute truth.

Our intellectual production has been so varied that we have often given the impression of being capricious and inconsistent. But what seems to outsiders like an inherent love of change is really nothing but the extreme rapidity with which the French mind deduces the consequences from the facts. If sometimes we appear revolutionary, it is because we never stop in the race for progress. We make discoveries; we publish them to the world; and, while others verify and apply them, we, availing ourselves of the start gained, are already perceiving their weak points and beginning the quest of something better which shall light another beacon along the road of knowledge. Our rapid progress, the facility with which we reject to-day's truth in favor of to-morrow's, is as surely a demonstration of the activity of our minds as of our originality.

Even when our writers do not lead the way, it is to them that people turn in order to grasp an idea originated by some other nation. Because we think and write clearly, our language is a marvelous instrument for the extension of knowledge. It is not without reason that the nations have adopted it in their diplomatic relations. It will always be the most convenient medium for the exchange of ideas. Indeed, we have often played the part of universal interpreter. We excel in extracting the best essential elements from foreign civilizations; and after having meditated on what we have found, after having developed and clarified it, we give it back to the world in a form so striking and lucid that the idea takes on the appearance of a revelation. What German philosopher was it who admitted that he did not fully understand the implications of his own concepts until his theories had been translated or interpreted by a Frenchman? Nor is that a mere quip. Our process of classifying, combining, and presenting the ideas of others often does actually contain an element of re-creation. Cuvier did not exaggerate when he said: "It is not through partiality that this report gives French savants the highest rank in nearly every one of the natural sciences. Foreigners concur in our estimate. And even in the branches in which chance has not ordained that the French should make the chief discoveries, the manner in which they have received, examined, and developed these discoveries and explored all their consequences places our compatriots very close to the original inventors, and in many respects gives them the right to share in their fame."[2]

To be in the vanguard of the conquering army of ideas, or even to bring new or beautiful ideas within the grasp of the general public, is assuredly a fine title to glory. Yet this is not, in my opinion, the highest honor which France can claim. Merely to admit our intellectual supremacy is not to do us full justice. What constitutes the value of French influence, indeed, is less the importance or the newness of the ideas advanced than our insistence upon the infinite value of the idea itself. I have already said, but must repeat—for I am referring here to the essential quality of our race—that we are preëminently the people who worship intelligence. As Mr. Orth said: "The Englishman honors the athlete, the German the soldier, the American the great business man; the Frenchman reserves his laurels for the man of intellect."[3] Indeed, we idolize everything pertaining to the mind—all that Guez de Balzac called "the voluptuous joys of reason and the delights of the intelligence"; and if we do not go quite so far as to find in them our whole happiness, at least we rate them far above material gratifications.

Only note, for example, our indifference to the refinements of comfort. This trait often astonishes you; it even makes you pity us a little. During the war I had many chances to converse with your soldiers. Even those of them who belonged to the poorer classes were amazed—to abandon polite euphemism, they were disgusted—not to find in universal use more of those little contrivances which admittedly make life easy and agreeable: electric light, telephones, central heating, and the like. And from this lack they concluded that France must be, not to desire these perfections of modern skill, a most benighted country. I had a good deal of difficulty in making them understand that that was in itself a proof of the uniquely advanced state of our civilization. Nothing is easier than to install a telephone in a house; all you need is a workman and a little money. But true civilization does not consist in striving after mere material progress; it consists in the life of the mind, in the greater and greater satisfaction of the loftiest aspirations. Whoever pays too much attention to this wretched body of ours loses sight of the needs of the soul—and, by the same token, whoever subordinates everything to the ambitions of the soul will not feel whatever discomforts the body may have to undergo. The French hate to do without luxury, which appeals to their artistic instincts, but they undergo privations without a murmur; they can live with contentment in badly heated houses and take a ten minutes' walk to carry their own messages. They are, as Mrs. Wharton very justly says, "an ascetic nation."[4]

The Frenchman is, then, in spite of appearances, essentially idealistic. Just as behind the skepticism of a few we easily descry the inward piety of all, so there coexists with French rationalism the unshakable belief that it is possible to realize a more and more perfect ideal of the Beautiful, the True, and the Good—one which will ultimately lift the race. I will go even farther: our idealism is, to use a mathematical expression, the very function of our rationalism, for it is by a more and more subtle use of the intelligence that we hope to arrive at the discovery of perfection, the only goal which makes life worth living. And, despite all setbacks, despite bitter disillusionments, we go on pursuing our chimera, incessantly subjecting our theories to a rigid scrutiny, and justifying these beautiful verses written by one who really understood the rôle of France, Elizabeth Barrett Browning:

> This poet of nations, who dreams on
> And wails on (while the household goes to wreck)
> For ever after some ideal Good.[5]

It is easy to disentangle the principal elements of the French ideal. That ideal rests essentially on belief in justice—the impersonal justice that must enable us to realize the lofty ends of our aspiration. As M. Fouillée remarks, France has always worshiped "pure, ideal, and universal justice"—justice founded on the sentiment of human dignity and universal equality. "When all is said, France formulated in her codes the most essential rules of civil justice. She tried to realize political justice in her constitutions by recognizing the government of all by all as the only legitimate method. And even in international relations, through the doctrines of her thinkers and the governing ideas of her masses, if not through the practice of her rulers or of all who have exploited her aspirations to their own profit, France has diligently sought justice and the brotherhood of nations. In the words of Guizot, 'She has often needed, in her own interests, to be reminded of her rights, because she has honored and loved abstract right above all else.' "[6]

Therein, France is the antithesis of those nations whose only criterion has been might. But do not suppose that our love of justice is animated merely by an intellectual impulse. Intermingled with our reasoning there is something emotional and impassioned—a sort of hatred of violence—kindled by an overwhelming pity for the feeble, the oppressed. François Coppée related an anecdote which I must tell you, because it gives a particularly vivid illustration of the aversion to brutality and the warmth of compassion which are at the root of all our revolts against injustice. In his *Souvenirs d'un Parisien* he narrates how his father used to tell his children stories in the evening.

"One particular story," the poet adds, "so deeply affected me that the Sandman himself was put to flight. It was the terrifying fable of the Wolf and the Lamb. Everyone must grant the unspeakable ferocity of this apologue—a thing worthy of Bismarck himself. Surely the tiny thing that I was at that time could not have understood the inexorable moral; but my awakening sensibilities found the brief tragedy unbearable. When my father adopted a gruff voice on reaching the words, '*Qui te rend si hardi de troubler mon breuvage?*' and, knowing the end of the story, I realized that the poor lamb was to defend itself in vain and presently be eaten up, I could bear it no longer. With my two little hands I would try to shut the mouth which was uttering those frightful words, and bursting into tears I would cry 'Not the wolf! Not the wolf!'

"At this desperate appeal my father would stop and console me with caresses, covering my hot, tear-stained cheeks with kisses. But I would see him smile; and I sometimes wondered what pleasure it could give him, good man that he was, to frighten a little child. For he insisted on telling me the horrible fable again, and I used to be almost angry with him for it, always trembling from the very start, always crying out at the same place: 'Not the wolf, Papa! Not the wolf!'

"Since those days I have understood why my father smiled to see me cry; he was pleased—gentle dreamer that he was!—pleased to see a first generous instinct germinating in the heart of his son; and he would persist, and go on to repeat the cruel masterpiece, that he might excite in me that sentiment so rare among children, pity. Be at rest, beloved father! Your lesson was not in vain, and those childish tears shed for La Fontaine's ill-fated lamb doubtless played their part in the formation of my mind and character. Be at rest! I shall never forget that scene of my childhood! and the poet who is your son still loves the weak and oppressed, just as he still hates injustice and tyranny.'"

What French child has not felt, the first time he read La Fontaine's fable, that same impulsive desire to fly to the rescue of the lamb? The impulse to take the part of the weak, even to glorify weakness rather than strength, is a very old sentiment, ingrained in our very fiber. We find it throbbing in the *Chanson de Roland,* the first great poem to express the French temperament. Angellier—a poet of great gifts who ought to be better known, for his verses are as vigorous as well-grown ears of wheat from fertile soil; he was, moreover, a first-rate critic—speaks of it thus: "The second characteristic which distinguishes the *Chanson de Roland* from other epics is that it possesses the supreme beauty of extolling misfortune, of making defeat noble and death glorious. Wherever I turn my eyes I see mankind celebrating victory and immortalizing strength . . . that is why it is an honor for this land to have produced an author who, with sublime courage and tenderness, sang of defeat and glorified a vanquished hero. For assuredly our history was not lacking in victories or in successful warriors. And it is one of our country's added glories that she has brought forth other men capable of admiring, loving, and ratifying this magnanimous choice. I know of nothing greater or more stirring than the wonderful way in which a nation free to choose at will among triumphant and glorious memories waxes enthusiastic over an epic of calamity and proudly venerates the memory of a defeat."[8] "France has substituted for the barbarous *Vae Victis* of antiquity the beautiful and noble *Gloria Victis*," says M. Nyrop. And this same Danish scholar points out that a *Gloria Victis* is to be found even in our national anthem, the *Marseillaise*. "In this hymn of liberty, this passionate song of patriotism and of a holy hatred of violence and tyranny, there is one stanza, often omitted, which reads:

>   *Français en guerriers magnanimes,*
>   *Portez et retenez vos coups,*
>   *Épargnez ces tristes victimes*
>   *À regret s'armant contre nous;*

>   Frenchmen, like warriors of generous hearts
>   Deal and withhold your blows:
>   Spare wretches duped by alien arts
>   Who hate to be your foes;

—that is to say, one ought to be merciful to foreign hireling soldiers who had invaded the country and made war on the Republic. That thought is typical. In what other national anthem is there a similar appeal for clemency to the enemy?"[9]

Perhaps this is no great credit to us, for we take pleasure in being a chivalrous nation. As early as the time of our ancestors, the Gauls, this was manifest. The German Mommsen recognized as much when he said: "They resembled Vercingetorix, their hero; they were gallant, they fought for liberty, they respected their plighted word, they died to keep their oaths. The dominating fact about them was that they were knights."[10] And when, with the Middle Ages, there arose the chivalric ideal, it was in France that it found its most perfect development, its most ardent expression. The ideas of sacrifice, honor, and disinterestedness which made up the creed of the *parfait gentil* knight of the time precisely corresponded with the virtues and devoirs calculated to capture the mind of the Frenchman. The triumph of these ideas, the prestige with which our people invested them, throws those bygone ages of our history into a clear and commanding relief.

This chivalric ideal we have guarded like a precious treasure through all the transformations which our manners have undergone, sometimes even carrying it to an extreme lest its hold weaken. So jealously have we guarded it, indeed, that we, the reasonable and reasoning nation *par excellence,* often do not reason at all about this. In acts to be performed, we have come to see not so much the necessity or the consequences as the comeliness of the attitude and expression with which they are accompanied. The end to be attained seems to us to be all the more desirable in proportion as the value of the act is imaginary and the profit to be gained by it problematical. To act for the pleasure of accomplishing a rare action, just for the glory of the thing, without thinking of comfort or well-being; to fight for a lost cause, simply because to do so enables us to gauge our capacity for sacrifice—that is what irresistibly attracts a Frenchman. Let us admit it; we love the *"panache."* When this word stands for a bombastic attitude, it is used in a derogatory sense. In its real and inner meaning, it implies nothing boastful or vainglorious. It merely describes that state of mind in which the chivalric spirit, intoxicated with its own ardor, becomes transcendent and attains to a sort of delirium of nobility. Rostand gave a wonderful definition of the *"panache"* in his *Cyrano de Ber-*

gerac. You remember the scene in which the hero draws his sword against imaginary enemies; and when those around him remonstrate, he cries:

> *Que dites-vous? . . . C'est inutile? . . . Je le sais!*
> *Mais on ne se bat point dans l'espoir du succès!*
> *Non! Non! C'est bien plus beau lorsque c'est inutile.*

> What's that you say? 'Tis bootless, eh? Why, yes.
> But when was fight mere foretaste of success?
> No, no! The one brave gesture is the vain.

And at the end of the play this same Cyrano, feeling Death's approach, cries:

Oui, vous m'arrachez tout, le laurier et la rose!
Arrachez! Il y a malgré vous quelque chose
Que j'emporte, et ce soir, quand j'entrerai chez Dieu,
Mon salut balayera largement le seuil bleu,
Quelque chose que sans un pli, sans une tache,
J'emporte malgré vous, et c'est . . . C'est? . . . Mon panache!

Ay, snatch it all—the laurel and the rose!
Take them! Yet, do your worst, there's something goes
With me; and when, this night, I'm passing through
God's door, my flourish sweeps his threshold blue
With that same something, pure and proud and fine
As ever. What, you ask?—This plume of mine!

When this play appeared, I, like all the young æsthetes of my generation, greeted its success with a disdainful smile. I accused Rostand of having cheapened his art by playing to the gallery. To-day, seeing things more impartially, I am forced to make amends; to recognize that *Cyrano* depicted, to say the least of it, one side of our national temper. The play aroused such tremendous enthusiasm because it touched the most vibrant chord in the French nature: its extravagant worship of heroism—a trait which has often cost us dear, but which is on that account none the less one of the most powerful spurs to French energy as well as the source of some of our noblest political inspirations.

It is a love of the *"panache"* which, throughout our history, has made us seek the path of hard duties and disinterested actions. How often have we fought for an idea! Indeed, it is in such a cause that we fight best. Witness the crusades—"those heroic manifestations of Christian idealism."[11] To wrest the tomb of Christ from the infidel—was there ever so lofty and yet so mad an idea? It was conceived by Frenchmen; if the Crusades drew together all nations in the same mystic impulse, it was in France that the movement started. M. Luchaire could say truthfully that "the first Crusade is France herself on the march."[12] A French Pope originated it; a French monk preached it and prepared men's minds for the heroic enterprise.

The Crusades and their exaltation are now far away in the dim ages of the past; no one to-day speaks of fighting for a sepulcher. And yet we are still Crusaders. The poet Charles Péguy was right when, in his *Mystère des Saints Innocents,* he made God say:

Les Français, comme ils sont, sont mes meilleurs serviteurs;
Ils ont été, ils seront toujours mes meilleurs soldats de la croisade.
 Or, il y aura toujours la croisade.[13]

The French, and no others, I call the best of my servants;
It is they who have been, and are ever, the soldiers of my
   crusade.
(And ah! my crusade is for ever.)

Our modern crusades have been wars undertaken in the defense of losing causes. We are impelled to sacrifice ourselves with all the more joy if our sacrifice appear useless. This characteristic of ours was noted with great acumen by an old historian of the time of Henry IV. Jérôme Bignon said: "To take up arms in one's own defence, for one's own ends, and to avenge one's injuries, is a thing as natural as it is common. But to take up arms for another who is wronged; to avenge him out of zeal for justice, without ulterior aims; to restore him to the place whence he has been driven—that is, beyond argument, a trait of really heroic virtue. . . . This trait has always been natural to the French."[14] Whenever a people has struggled for freedom against a foreign oppression, we have rushed to their aid, urged by an instinctive and irresistible impulse.

We once tried to help a young Republic which, in her weakness, was endeavoring to shake off the dominion of the most powerful of empires. I hope you will not see, in what I am about to say, a tactless reminder of services rendered. But to-day we can speak frankly. Your soldiers have now, in turn, given their blood to save France; you have paid a hundred-fold the debt contracted long ago—a debt which we, moreover, had forgotten. There is no longer any question of creditor or debtor. We can, then, without ulterior design or fear of being misunderstood, dwell candidly on that common history in which the roots of the friendship between the United States and France are deeply planted.

Some who have watched the progress of this friendship have muttered angrily: "The French were glad enough to play a trick on the English: their own interest demanded it." Well, no doubt a trace of willingness to embarrass the nation which we had always found opposing our development was mingled, whether admittedly or no, with the sympathy which we felt for you. But do you believe that so base a sentiment would have been enough to explain the enthusiasm which took possession of all France and made her project herself bodily into the most perilous of adventures? For, I would have you note, if we had but listened to our national egoism, every consideration would have forbidden us to meddle in your affairs. To begin with, we had no reason to love you. The colonies in revolt were formed in part of countries discovered by our explorers and subsequently wrested from us. Your general-in-chief was that same Washington who in 1753 had ordered the French to evacuate Ohio, where they had established themselves, and who in the following year had exterminated the troops commanded by Jumonville. We even had, you see, some reasons for bearing you a grudge. Our financial condition, moreover, was desperate. We were heavily burdened with debts; any new expense might lead to bankruptcy. And it was precisely because the king and his minister, Vergennes, knew the peril that they refused at first to engage in a war against England. But the chivalrous spirit of the nation was stronger than the prudence of the politicians. What the responsible heads of the government could not in con-

THE MISSION OF FRANCE

science undertake, private individuals who listened only to their hearts were able to accomplish. We could not endure in inaction the thought of a weak people fighting against a great power. We wanted to be where hard blows were being struck for a just cause which seemed imperiled.

Among the French friends of the "rebels" there was one in particular to whom justice ought to be rendered. You have slightly forgotten him. In these days when you make it a point of honor to draw from the pigeon-holes of your desks the I.O.U.'s of your most insignificant ancient debts, I have not once heard his name mentioned. Yet he played one of the most important rôles in the history of your independence. The man I mean is Beaumarchais. His intentions were often misrepresented, not only in America, but also in France. People persisted in detecting a personal interest where, as all the documents go to prove, there was nothing but passionate generosity. The author of the *Mariage de Figaro,* even if he wanted legitimate reimbursement for the considerable sums expended in your cause, was none the less inspired by a most genuine enthusiasm for that cause. The matter of money certainly came second to the wish to serve. Speaking of the sums which he had lent to an officer, M. de Steuben, to enable him to join your armies, Beaumarchais wrote: "Never have I used money so as to give me more happiness. . . . I learn that he is Inspector General of all the American forces: bravo! Tell him that his glory is the interest on my money."[15] Again, he wrote to Silas Deane, on the 22d of July, 1776, "I mean to serve your country as if it were my own, and I hope to find in the friendship of a generous people the true reward of labors gladly consecrated to their cause.'"[16] He took it upon himself to be your advocate in France; he overwhelmed the king with reports in your favor. You were in a critical situation. Poorly equipped, outnumbered, you had already lost several battles against the British troops. All Europe was convinced that you were lost. But Beaumarchais believed in your victory; and he communicated his confidence to those around him. He did better: he helped you to turn the tide of fortune. You lacked arms and powder; your armies were half-naked. He eventually succeeded in obtaining secretly from the Minister, Vergennes, a loan of a million and the authorization to borrow arms and munitions from the national arsenals. At the risk of ruining himself, he spent his whole fortune in supplies to be sent to you. Eluding the suspicious eye of the British ambassador, he collected an enormous amount of material in various ports—two hundred field pieces, mortars, bombs, bullets, twenty-five thousand rifles, two hundred thousand barrels of powder. He had clothing and camp equipment made for twenty-five thousand men.[17] And when you failed to come promptly to take possession of these aids, he chartered vessels and armed them. He enrolled officers, lent them money, and, surmounting a thousand obstacles, succeeded in slipping his vessels out under the very nose of the British ambassador, who, at last getting wind of the affair, was remonstrating fruitlessly with our government. Do you suppose for a minute that the merely retaliatory satisfaction of harassing the English is enough to account for the stubbornness of Beaumarchais?

And do you suppose for a minute that hatred of

England accounts for the part played by Lafayette? I was not going to mention his name, if only because it is the regular thing to mention it. But how, recalling this all-important crisis of your history, can one help speaking of him? On the 26th of April, 1777, when he set out, he was just twenty years old. He was married to a young and beautiful woman whom he tenderly loved. His whole family was opposed to his project of going to fight for you. The king explicitly forbade him to go. He would listen to nothing —not to his wife's pleading, not to his family's reproaches, not to the king's commands. He bought a vessel in secret and set sail, saying in self-justification, "As soon as I understood the quarrel, my heart was enlisted, and I could think of nothing except joining the colors which I had come to think of as my own." Lafayette's fine action was the signal which unleashed public enthusiasm. Volunteers swarmed to the side of the gallant gentleman who had so nobly dedicated himself to the cause of right. The king and Vergennes, carried away at last by the public enthusiasm, signed the Treaty of Alliance, toward which they had been secretly leaning without daring to admit it. America was saved!

Nor are you the only country which we have aided in its struggle for liberty. In 1827 we took the part of Greece against the Turks. Every illustrious Frenchman declared himself on the side of the nation which was so resolutely asserting its independence. The Philhellenic Committee of Paris assembled money, arms, and men, and the government put its resources at the disposal of the War of Liberation. Our sailors were at Navarino; our troops, landing in Morea, gave the fatal blow to

Turkish power. In 1830 we helped Belgium free herself from Holland; it was a French army which saved the Belgian forces when they were about to be crushed, and which liberated Antwerp and the mouths of the Scheldt. In 1859 Napoleon the Third constituted himself the founder of Italian unity. An ardent partisan of the principle of nationalism, the emperor made it his mission to restore to the descendants of the Latins the place in Europe which was theirs by right. If the Sardinian Kingdom is to-day the Kingdom of Italy, that is due, indeed, to the determination of its people; but it is also due in great part to the French victories of Magenta and Solferino. Even German unity owes something to us, for Napoleon, somewhat quixotically, encouraged the entente between Prussia and Italy—an entente which was presently to facilitate the birth of the German Empire. Yes, we have often shown the world the spectacle of a nation forgetting its own interest and safety, whenever the well-being of others is endangered.

It is a fact proved by our whole history that France has never considered human happiness except under the aspect of universal happiness. We think, not in terms of the nation, but in terms of the world. "With a truth useful to my country alone," said Montesquieu, "I would have nothing to do." For us, there is no such thing as progress which cannot and ought not to be enjoyed in common by every nation. Our thinking has always been, in essence as in expression, cosmopolitan. Ever since there were any French writers, our authors have addressed themselves to the study of mankind—not merely mankind in their own country, but mankind of every time and clime. It is in behalf of universal man that they have built up, independently of frontiers, their dreams of perfection; and whenever they thought they had discovered the truth so long sought, they knew no rest until they had made it benefit the rest of the world.

Is not this world-embracing altruism the most striking feature of the French Revolution? From the very outset France aimed beyond her own frontiers. She endeavored to emancipate, not the French alone, but all mankind. Our ancestors believed with all their hearts that the Rights of Man were for all men, all countries, all ages. "For," as André Chénier said in his *Avis au Peuple Français,* "one should not lose sight of the fact that France is not, at this moment, entrusted with her own interests merely: the cause of all Europe is in her hands. The Revolution which has just taken place among us is, as it were, pregnant with the destinies of the world. The surrounding nations have their eyes fixed on us; they await the result of our internal conflicts with interested impatience and anxious curiosity; and one may say that the human race is now occupied in making, in our persons, a great experiment. If we succeed, the fate of Europe is changed. Men regain their rights; peoples win back their usurped sovereignty; kings struck by the success of our labors and warned by the example of the King of the French, may reach a compromise with the nations whom they are called to govern; and it may be that more fortunate peoples, profiting by our lesson, will attain to a just and liberal constitution without passing through the troubles and calamities which led us to this beginning of all blessings. Then liberty will spread and propagate in every way, and the name of France will be blessed throughout the world!"[18] Such were the ideas, made up of love, charity, and self-sacrifice, which sustained our volunteers of 1792 and lent them an irresistible energy. They were convinced that, by dying for their country, they were "emancipating the human race" and bringing happiness together with brotherhood upon the whole world.

A wonderful dream, and one which we have tirelessly pursued. From century to century voices have been raised among us for the formation of a society —give it what name you will, whether United States of the World or Society of Nations—in which all men, made one by love and oblivious of frontiers, should form a single people, every unit living in amity and brotherly affection. Henry IV conceived the idea of a general Republic of Christianity. Gentle Fénelon, caustic Montesquieu, sentimental Bernardin de Saint-Pierre, sanguine Condorcet, fiery Mirabeau—all our romantic socialists from Saint-Simon to Edgar Quinet—have, each according to his temperament, outlined this international society which was to pave the way to eternal peace. A wonderful dream which all Frenchmen sincerely long to see realized, even though they remember that a too firm belief therein has often in time past put them at the mercy of peoples less generous and less simple-hearted.

Let us not regret our disinterestedness. It is the strength and the contagious virtue of our civilization. If the nations are willing to come to us, if they trust us and learn of us, it is because they know that they will not have to cope with selfish policies, based on the interests of our country alone. Rather, they find in our eternal search for progress, in the solutions which we formulate, the satisfaction of their own aspirations, an anticipation of their own desires. France appears to them in the guise of an elder sister—a solicitous and loving sister who takes care of the younger ones, experiments in their behalf, voluntarily sacrifices herself to spare them life's shocks, and guides them by her example toward the ideal of grace, justice, and liberty which she has set for herself.

In other words, it is the mission of France to ally her own development to the destiny of civilization. All nations beheld the sudden revelation of this fact when, in 1914, our very existence was imperilled. You remember it well—how, when in August of that terrible year people learned that the Germans were marching on Paris, were under its very walls, the whole world was in an agony of apprehension. Even those who thought they had grievances against us felt the dejection which accompanies great catastrophes. It was then that they saw what France meant to them and how much poorer they would themselves be for her loss. And their fears were not empty. Had France been crushed, the world would have continued to revolve on its axis and the sun to give heat—true. People would also have gone on loving and hating and struggling for interests or for ideas. But one of the shining stars would have disappeared from the firmament of man; and it is well within the truth to say that humanity would not have advanced with so sure a footing on the hazardous road to truth and light.

Notes

Chapter I

[1] Vidal de la Blache: *Tableau de la géographie de la France* (in E. Lavisse: *Histoire de la France*, Paris, 1900-1911, I, 1, 31).

[2] J. Brunhes: *Géographie humaine de la France* (in G. Hanotaux: *Histoire de la nation française des origines préhistoriques jusqu'à nos jours*. Paris, 1920 ff.), I, 108.

[3] Receptacles for holding water or oil with which to mix the paints.

[4] J. Brunhes: *Géographie humaine de la France* (vide supra), I, 112-113.

[5] C. Jullian: *Histoire de la Gaule* (Paris, 1908 ff.), I, 110.

[6] *Timagène*, in *Ammien Marcellin*, XV, 9, 4.

[7] J. Brunhes: *Géographie humaine de la France* (vide supra), I, 124.

[8] J. Brunhes: *Géographie humaine de la France* (vide supra), I, 125.

[9] Some historians maintain that southern Gaul was already occupied by Iberians when this invasion occurred.

[10] C. Jullian: *Histoire de la Gaule*, I, 255-256.

[11] J. Brunhes: *Géographie humaine de la France* (vide supra), I, 124.

[12] C. Jullian: *Histoire de la Gaule*, I, 319.

[13] Quoted by A. Fouillée in *Psychologie du peuple français* (Paris, 1898), 162 n.

[14] According to J. Brunhes (*Géographie humaine de la France*, I, 143), the Vandals and the Alani were of Slavic origin.

[15] J. E. Migne: *Patrum latinorum traditio catholica* (Paris, 1879), XXII, 1057-1058. The reader will doubtless have noticed that, in the history of the invasions of France, the same names constantly recur in the list of towns which have suffered. Rheims, Amiens, and Arras were focal points of the German vindictiveness in 1914, precisely as in the fifth century.

[16] J. Brunhes: *Géographie humaine de la France* (vide supra), I, 143. According to M. Brunhes, the Franks were not Germanic, but belonged to the tall, fair, dolichocephalic Nordic type of the Scandinavian group.

[17] Great numbers of them, however, remained in Septimania. The type to which they belonged still persists in parts of southern France

NOTES

—for instance, in the Gironde. *Cf.* J. Brunhes: *Géographie humaine de la France* (*vide supra*), I, 145.

[18] C. Jullian: *Histoire de la Gaule*, I, 112.

[19] G. Bloch, in Lavisse: *Histoire de la France*, I, ii, 102.

[20] N.-D. Fustel de Coulanges: *La Gaule romaine* (Paris, 1891), 137.

[21] "Itaque hoc jam diu est consecutus, ut, in quo quisque artificio excelleret, is in suo genere Roscius diceretur." Cicero: *De Oratore*, I, 28, 130.

[22] *Claudii Rutilii Namiatiani de reditu suo libri* II, i, 5-14.

[23] G. Dottin: *Anciens peuples de l'Europe* (Paris, 1916), 238.

[24] W. Z. Ripley: *Races of Europe* (London, 1900), 131.

[25] E. Renan: *Qu'est-ce qu'une nation?* in *Discours et Conférences* (Paris, 1887), 307.

[26] Vidal de la Blache: *Tableau de la géographie de la France* (*vide supra*), I, 22.

[27] Vidal de la Blache: *Tableau de la géographie de la France* (*vide supra*), I, 40.

Chapter II

[1] A. Fouillée: *Psychologie du peuple français*, 180.

[2] Letter of September 18, 1669.

[3] Letter of November 6, 1681.

[4] Montesquieu: *Esprit des Lois*, XIX, v.

[5] *A Journey to France* (London, 1826), 171.

[6] C. Lenient: *La comédie au xviiie siècle* (Paris, 1888), II, 275.

[7] Quoted by G. Deschamps in *Marivaux* (Paris, 1897), 84-85.

[8] V. du Bled: *Société française*, Série VIII (Paris, 1911), 254 ff.

[9] Voltaire: *Relation de la mort du Chevalier de La Barre*, in *Œuvres* (Ed. Garnier, Paris, 1879), XXV, 513-514.

[10] Quoted by V. Giraud in *La Troisième France* (Paris, 1917), 108.

[11] M. Barrès: *Les familles spirituelles de la France* (Paris, 1917), 112.

[12] *Parmi les ruines* (Paris, 1915), 377-378.

[13] E. Gomez Carillo: *Au cœur de la tragédie* (Paris, 1917), 78.

[14] Essay XXVI.

[15] *A Sentimental Journey*, Address at Versailles.

[16] *A Residence in France* (1836), II, 311.

[17] *The France of To-day* (London, 1916), 65.

[18] *The France of To-day* (London, 1916), 28.

[19] In Lavisse: *Histoire de la France* (*vide supra*), III, i, 368.

[20] *America To-day* (London, 1900), 73.

[21] V. Ch. Petit-Dutaillis, in Lavisse: *Histoire de la France* (*vide supra*), IV, ii, 115.

NOTES

Chapter III

[1] A. Fouillée: *Psychologie du peuple français* (*vide supra*), 183.

[2] *Outlines of Sociology* (London, 1898), 9.

[3] J. Th. Merz: *A History of European Thought in the Nineteenth Century* (second edition, London, 1904), Introduction, 75.

[4] M. Houllevigue (in *Civilisation française* for January 20, 1920, p. 160) disagrees as follows: "We have had a good many inventors whose genius for the practical, when addressed to problems of detail, has resulted in extending invention to the ultimate stages of its practical utility. Jacquard and his loom, Daguerre and photography, Pasteur and his vaccines, and, in our own day, Moissan and the electric oven, Claude and the fractional distillation of liquid air, Marius Latour, Boucherot and the electric motor, Rateau and the turbine, Maurice Leblanc and his refrigerating apparatus. . . ."

[5] E. Bouty, in *La Science Française* (Exposition universelle et internationale de San Francisco, Paris, 1915. 2 vols.), I, 133.

[6] Mallard, quoted in *La Science Française* (*vide supra*), I, 170.

[7] For further information, see *La Science Française* (*vide supra*).

[8] H. Bergson: *La philosophie*, in *La Science Française*, I, 31-32.

[9] H. Bergson: *La philosophie*, in *La Science Française*, I, 29.

[10] P. Bourget: *Essais de psychologie contemporaine* (Paris, 1883), 266.

[11] Claude Bernard expressed this conviction of the French when he asserted that "the human mind invariably functions syllogistically: it could get nowhere by any other process" (*Introduction à la médecine expérimentale*, 72. Paris, 1898).

[12] A. Luchaire, in Lavisse: *Histoire de la France*, II, ii, 380.

[13] G. Lanson: *Histoire de la littérature française* (fifth edition, Paris, 1898), 396.

[14] Art. XVI, 16.

[15] G. Lanson: *Histoire de la littérature française* (*vide supra*), 620.

[16] Quoted by Daniel Mornet in *Le romanticisme française*, in *Civilisation française* (November-December, 1919), 432.

[17] A. Fouillée: *Psychologie du peuple français* (*vide supra*), 187.

[18] *Cf.* Bertin: *Etudes sur la société française* (Paris, 1889), 45-46.

[19] A. Fouillée: *Psychologie du peuple français* (*vide supra*), 188-189.

[20] J. H. Fichte: *Sur les conditions d'un théisme spéculatif* (written on the occasion of Schelling's Preface to Cousin's *Philosophie française et allemande*, 1835). Reprinted in Fichte's *Introduction à la méthode pour arriver à la vie bienheureuse*, translated from the German by M. Bouillier, Paris, 1845.

NOTES

[21] *Cf.* Ch.-V. Langlois, in Lavisse: *Histoire de la France* (*vide supra*), III, ii, 380.

Chapter IV

[1] *French Traits* (New York, 1889), 252.
[2] *Molière* (New York, 1910), 328.
[3] *Imagination créatrice* (Paris, 1900), 269.
[4] It is, moreover, a very ancient French story. Bonaventure des Périers related it in *Les contes ou les nouvelles récréations et joyeux devis*, Nouvelle XIV; and Rabelais alluded to it (I, xxxiii).
[5] *De la connaissance des bons livres.* Quoted by P. V. Delaporte in *Le merveilleux dans la littérature française sous le regne de Louis XIV* (Paris, 1891), 44.
[6] Delaporte, *ibid.*, 70 ff.
[7] Galland's twelve-volume translation came out 1704-1717.
[8] *Histoire de la littérature française*, 1062.
[9] H. Matthey, *Essai sur le merveilleux dans la littérature française depuis 1800* (Paris, 1915), gives a long list of the nineteenth-century French writers who exploited mystery and wonder.
[10] *Essais de psychologie contemporaine*, 165.
[11] Ribot: *Imagination créatrice*, 140.
[12] Quoted by Ribot, *Imagination créatrice*, 210.
[13] P. Bourget: *Essais de psychologie*, 41.
[14] *Dix ans d'études historiques* (second edition, Paris, 1836), 16-17.
[15] Preface to *Bérénice*.
[16] *Poésies, "Stances et Poèmes"* (1865-1866), 210. (Paris, n.d.)
[17] Ribot: *Imagination créatrice*, 144.
[18] P. Bourget: *Nouveaux Essais*, 213.

Chapter V

[1] *Considérations sur les mœurs*, 4.
[2] *Soixante ans de souvenirs* (second edition, Paris), I, 86.
[3] *The France of To-day*, 148-149.
[4] P. Bourget: *Essais de psychologie*, 274.
[5] *Vie d'Henri Brulard*, ed. Champion (Paris, 1912), I, 192.
[6] *Lettres à l'Etrangère* (1842-1844; Paris, 1906), 141.
[7] Vol. II (London, 1782), 166.
[8] Lanson: *Littérature française*, 83.

NOTES

[9] *Nouveaux essais*, 51.

[10] Ch. Henry: *Correspondance inédite de Condorcet et de Turgot* (1770-1779; Paris, n.d.), 146.

[11] W. R. Lawrence: *Charities of France* (London, 1866), 14.

[12] *Ibid.*, 123.

[13] A. Feillet: *Misère au temps de la Fronde et Saint Vincent de Paul* (Paris, 1862), 256.

[14] *Cf.* Balch: *Public Assistance of the Poor in France*, in Publications of the American Economic Association, vol. VIII, 1893.

[15] The following are some of the principal French institutions which collaborate for the relief of poverty and amelioration of social conditions:—

(1) Institutions for the help of mothers and children. House visits for the oversight of infants; philanthropic societies for the oversight of workmen's housing conditions; medical examination; societies for physical education; vacation camps; canteens for school children; organizations of former pupils; students' benefit societies; benevolent societies; organizations of pupils' parents.—Aid to pregnant women; houses of refuge; workrooms for the pregnant; maternity homes; convalescent homes; maternity benefit societies; maternity canteens; baby clinics; nurseries; milk distribution; crèches; societies for the aid of mothers; societies to encourage the nursing of infants by their mothers; societies for protection of childhood; societies for the provision of layettes.

(2) Aids to the sick and the poor. Orphanages; old men's homes; hospitals for the incurably diseased; asylums for the insane; philanthropic organizations; free medical aid.—National institutions (Charenton, Quinze-Vingt) for blind children and deaf-mutes; the Vacassy Homes; convalescent hospitals (Vincennes, Vésinet). Community institutions; crèches; orphanages; night-shelters; dispensaries; sanatoria. Mutual benefit societies to the number of more than 22,000, with a combined membership of over 5,000,000.

(3) Preventive morality. An organization for the general oversight of prisons; societies for the protection of juvenile law-breakers; children's courts; societies for the rescue and help of juvenile delinquents; and many more. (*Cf.* P. Strauss: *L'Assistance*, in *Un demi-siècle de civilisation française*, Hachette, 1916, 403-420.)

[16] Art. XVI, 96.

[17] *Troisième Carnet* (Paris, 1915), 48.

NOTES

Chapter VI

[1] *French Traits*, 6.
[2] Volney: *Tableau du climat et du sol des États-Unis.* Quoted by Taine: *Origines de la France contemporaine* (Paris, 1885), "L'Ancien régime," 161.
[3] *French Home Life*, 264-267.
[4] *Psychologie du peuple français*, 160.
[5] Lanson: *Littérature française*, 368.
[6] *Ibid.*, 373.
[7] *Mémoires* (ed. Tourneux), II, 229.
[8] *Understanding the French* (New York, 1914), 221.
[9] Lanson: *Littérature française*, 372.
[10] Quoted by Lanson in *Littérature française*, 372.
[11] *French Home Life*, 255.
[12] *De L'Allemagne*, I, xi.
[13] *Caractères*, V.
[14] Mme. Campan: *Mémoires* (ed. Barrière), X, 47.
[15] *Mémoires* (ed. Tourneux), II, 82.
[16] *Soixante ans de souvenirs*, I, 352.
[17] *Caractères*, XII.
[18] Ch. 51.
[19] *Stances*, 28.
[20] Quoted by A. Babeau in *Voyageurs en France* (Paris, 1885), 248, 273.
[21] Marshall: *French Home Life*, 208.
[22] Cf. Lanson, *Idéal français dans la littérature*, viii, in *Civilisation française* for February, 1920, 109.
[23] *Understanding the French*, 111.
[24] *French Traits*, 11.

Chapter VII

[1] *The France of To-day*, 217-218.
[2] G. Lafenestre, *Molière* (Paris, 1909), 145.
[3] Lesage: *Histoire de Guzman d'Alfarache*, Translator's preface (Paris, 1815), I, vii.
[4] Preface to *La physiologie de l'amour moderne* (Paris, 1890).
[5] Quoted by Ferry in *Balzac et ses amies*, 63.
[6] Cf. *Annuaire Statistique de la France*, Vol. 34 (1914-1915), Tab. 5, p. 168.*
[7] *New International Encyclopædia* (New York, 1915), article on "Illegitimacy."

NOTES

8 *Encyclopædia Britannica*, eleventh edition, article on "Illegitimacy."
9 *Essais*, III, v.
10 *Cf*. Ch. Lefebvre: *La famille française dans le droit et dans les mœurs* (Paris, 1920), 94, 106-107.
11 *Soixante ans de souvenirs*, II, 54.
12 *Souvenirs d'un Parisien* (Paris, 1910), 16-19.
13 *The France of To-day*, 138.

Chapter VIII

1 E. H. Vollet: *France ecclésiastique* (in Grande Encyclopédie, Vol. XVII); E. Chenon: *Histoire des rapports de l'église et de l'état du premier au vingtième siècle* (Paris, 1913), II, ii; Bayet, in Lavisse: *Histoire de la France*, II, i, 216-217.
2 E. H. Vollet: *France ecclésiastique* (*vide supra*).
3 E. Chenon: *Histoire des rapports*, etc. (*vide supra*), 65-66.
4 E. H. Vollet: *France ecclésiastique* (*vide supra*).
5 E. Chenon: *Histoire des rapports*, etc. (*vide supra*), 103.
6 E. H. Vollet: *Gallicanisme* (in *Grande Encyclopédie*, Vol. XVIII).
7 Ch. Loyseau: *Traité des ordres* (second edition, 1665), ch. iii.
8 E. H. Vollet: *France ecclésiastique* (*vide supra*).
9 This lecture was delivered February 20, 1920.

Chapter IX

1 *French Traits*, 92.
2 *Rapport historique sur les progrès des sciences depuis 1789* (Paris, 1810), 391.
3 *Imperial Impulse*, 67.
4 Edith Wharton: *French Ways*, 135.
5 *Aurora Leigh*, VI, 55.
6 A. Fouillée: *France au point de vue morale* (Paris, 1900), 14-15.
7 *Souvenirs d'un Parisien*, 23.
8 A. Angellier: *Étude sur la Chanson de Roland* (Paris, 1878), 73-74.
9 Ch. Nyrop: *La France* (translated from the Danish, 1916), 25.
10 Quoted by C. Jullian in *La tradition française* (Paris, 1915), 27.
11 V. Giraud: *La civilisation française* (Paris, 1917), 43.
12 Lavisse, *Histoire de la France*, II, ii, 228.

Date Due			
FEB 1 2 '34			
MAR 2 '36			
MAR 31 '36			
DEC 11 '40			
FEB 25 '42			
APR 5 '43			
MAR 24 '45			
NOV 6 '62			
NOV 8 '62			
OCT 10 '63			
DEC 3 '64			
NOV 4 '65			
JAN			
DEC 11 1975			
MAR 30 1983			

INDEX

156: reasons for opposing neutrality and supporting Franco-British coalition, 147; belief in constitutional monarchy, 149; identification with Republic, 149 ff.; motion to impeach, and attempt on life of, 153; supposed knowledge of mutiny, 155 f.; King George's coöperation with, 163; death, 168, 169

Veto, legislative, within power of King, 101

Victoria, Queen, 112

Voting, see Franchise

VouIgaris, Demetrios, 111, 113; ministry headed by, 141

War of Independence, internecine strife attending, 13; intellectual preparation, 18, 20; neutrality of Ionian Islands, 27; conditions resulting from effect of self-government under Ottoman rule, 33; see also Insurrection; Revolution

William of Denmark, Prince, called to throne, 128; elected, 130; see also George I, King

World War, issues engendered by, 3, 5; legal basis for intervention of powers during, 132; divergence of opinion of entry into, 140; political and constitutional crisis precipitated by, 140–47; 148

Young Turks, 5, 137

Ypsilantis, Alexander, 41, 43, 64n

Ypsilantis, Demetrios, 36, 37n, 46: objectives and work of, 43-45; made president, 44; as a military leader, 44, 45; reasons for political eclipse, 45; legislature under, 53

Zaïmis, Alexander, 142, 150, 154, 155, 162, 169

Zaïmis, Andrew, 50

Zavitsanos, Constantine, 169

Zosimadaï brothers, 11

187

Russia (*Continued*)
dismemberment in plan of, 39; unwarranted reliance on, 41, 42; Capodistrias in service of, 59, 60–64; position re Othonian regime, 103, 114; recalls Minister in Athens, 107; development of policy during insurrection of 1862, 118 ff.; policy during World War, 144; *see also* Protecting powers
Russo-Turkish war, influence of, 84

Sacred Law, 9, 28
St. Petersburg Protocol of April 4, 1826, 81, 118
Saripolos, N. N., cited, 135
Schools, secular influence, 10; *see also* Education
Sectional government in unitary state, 48, 56
Self-government, conditional, under Ottoman rule, 27–33; Capodistrias's system of provincial administration, 78; surrender for in-dependence from Ottoman rule, 80–95
Senate, Peloponnesian, 44, 45; American, 49; abolition of Greek, 154, 157, 158
Separation of powers, 47, 49, 52, 73
Sèvres, Treaty of, 5, 148
Shipowning class, 42, 46, 49
Simopoulos, M., 162
Skouloudis, Stephen, 142
Skyfakakis, Colonel, 169
Sophoulis, Themistocles, 166
Sovereignty, forfeiture of, in exchange for independence from Ottoman rule, 80–95; exercise of the constituent power the primary manifestation of, 85; transferred from nation to monarch, 90, 92; of Crown affirmed by Bavaria, 93; primacy of national, affirmed under monarchy, 130, 132; self-limitation through Constitution of 1864, 135
Spezzia, 48, 49, 54
Stratos, M. A., 160n
Stratos, Nicholas, 160n
Submission, Act of, 39, 81
Succession to throne, 107
Suffrage, *see* Franchise

"Supreme Authority" preached by *Philiké*, 43
Switzerland, Capodistrias's mission to, 59, 60–62

Tax payment, 29, 31
Theotokis, George, 24
Theotokis, John, 166
Thessaly, Eastern, 30
Tilsit agreements, 27, 60
Treaties: immutability of, upheld, 132 (*see also* Conventions)
— Nov. 5, 1815, 27
— July 6, 1827, 40, 58, 81, 82, 84
— May 7, 1832, 91, 92, 105, 107, 108, 109, 113, 117, 125, 126, 128, 131, 132
— Nov. 20, 1852, 108, 117, 122, 126
— July, 1863, 131
— March 29, 1864, 131
Treaty-making power, 99
Treaty of Amiens, 26
Treaty of Sèvres, 5, 148
Tricoupis, Charilaos, 141
Tricoupis, S., 77, 93, 97, 112, quoted, 66
Troezene, Constitution of, 58, 68, 71, 72, 73; provisions, 51 f.
Troppau, Congress of, 62
Tsaldaris, Premier, 151, 152, 153, 157, 158, 159, 161, 162, 165, 166, 168; resignation, 152; death, 168, 169
Turkey, property transferred by, 171; frustration of its last attempt to limit Greek sovereignty, 94, 109; deportation of Greek subjects of, 171; *see also* Ottoman Empire

Unitary state, recommended by Jefferson, 17; efforts to establish, 43, 51, 67; postulated by first constitution, 46; sectionalism in, 48; justification for, 56
"United States of the Ionian Islands," 27; *see also* Ionian Islands

Vaulgaris, Count, quoted, 65n, 68n
Venetian Empire, Ionian control, 23, 24, 26
Venizelos, Eleutherios, struggle between Constantine and, 5, 140 ff., 148, 149; as adviser to Military League, 138; first government, 139; interventionist policy, 145 ff., 148.

INDEX

tervention, 105, 132; interference and dictation intensified, 108; dictation on financial policy, 109; construe guarantee as safeguard for bondholders, 110; development of policy during Insurrection of 1862, 116 ff.; policies during World War crisis, 144 ff.; dependence on, and its end, 171 f.
Protocols, of March 22, 1829, 84; of April 4, 1826, 81; 118; of Feb. 3, 1830, 69, 71, 80, 84, 94, 124, 128, 134
Provincial administration, "provisional" system of Capodistrias, 78
Provincial autonomy, 29, 55, 56
Provisional Electoral Law, 54, 78
Psara, 48, 54

Radical Union, 166
Reaction, vs. revolution, 35; democracy and, 170
Reason, age of, 11
Refugees, influx of, 6, 148; sympathies, 149; deportation of Greek subjects of Turkey, 171
Regency, King of Bavaria authorized to establish, 91; attitude toward constitution and sovereignty of people, 93; provision for temporary, 99; constitutional provisions, 107
Religion, as only line of cleavage among Ottoman subjects, 33; of monarch, 108, 122, 126, 130, 131
Repas, Colonel, 162
Representative government, acquaintance with, 33; see also Constitutionalism
Republic of 1924–25, establishment of, 6, 149; whether new Greek state would be monarchy or, 38; identified with Venizelos, 149; foreign policy, 149 ff.; Constitution, 150, 157; dependence on Liberal Party, 151; placed in keeping of anti-Venizelists, 157 f.; anti-Venizelist campaign in defense of, 160; abolition of, 162; result of plebiscite, 162 f.; radical reorientation of foreign policy under, 171
Republicans vs. royalists, 150 ff., 157
Revenue, raising of, under Ottoman rule, 29

Revolution, obstructed by Greek preoccupation with politics, 33; constitutional experiments, 34–37; course pursued on question of the monarchy, 37; shipowners the financial bulwark of, 42; nadir of, marked by disastrous phase of civil war, 50; conservatism, administrative system, 55 ff.; election of assemblies, 75; political principles of, adapted to monarchical government, 88; first crisis a revolt against Otho's autocratic government, 96; longest cycle in history of Modern Greece, 140; see also Insurrection; War of Independence
Revolutionary agitation of Rhigas, 19 ff.
Revolutionary movements, European awareness of implications of, 35; opposition of Capodistrias to, 59, 64; Rhigas of Velestinos, 10; execution, 18n; opinions and career, 18–22; writings, 19 ff., 22n; chief aim, 22; secret society inheriting tradition of, 41
"Romaic Nation," 27, 28, 29, 31
Roman Catholics, civil and religious liberty, 80, 134
Romanofsky, Prince, 122
Rouphos, A., 113
Rouphos, M., 164
Rousseau, Jean Jacques, 13, 21
Royalists vs. Republicans, 150 ff., 157; obtain possession of Republic, 157; influence, 158; plebiscite, 162 f.
Royalist Union, 159
Ruling class, merchants, 10, 11, 42, 46; landowning oligarchy, 14, 26, 32, 41, 42, 54; hostility to hereditary aristocracy 14, 59, 64, 67, 77; dominance by aristocracy, 23, 24, 26; primates, 32; attitude toward Philikē, 41, 42; toward the Insurrection, 42 f.; shipowners, 42, 46, 49; compromise with, and offer presidency to Ypsilantis, 44
Russell, John, 115; position on Insurrection of 1862, 116 ff.
Russia, treaty "guarantees," the legal basis for intervention of, 6; Koraes's attitude toward, 17; occupation of Ionian Islands, 25, 59; menace of

185

INDEX

Otho, King (*Continued*)
throughout, 102, 111, 113; Russian hostility to, 103; attitude of powers toward, 103 ff., 114 ff.; abandons pretense of constitutional government, 111 f.; question of family rights to throne, 127; *see also* Monarchy

Othoneos, General, 152

Ottoman Empire, conditional self-government under, 4, 9, 27–33; attainment of independence from, 6; decay of, and changes in Greek consciousness and conditions, 9; lack of a basic cultural unity, 19; Ionian freedom from rule of, 23; method of dealing with non-Moslem subjects, 27; rule in the Peloponnesus, 30–33; government after freedom from rule of, 34 ff., 56; insurgency against, irrevocable, 43; property of, confiscated, 66; suzerainty accepted by Greeks, 82; payment of compensation to, 82, 92; effects of Russo-Turkish war, 84; forced to subscribe to decisions of London Conference, 84; Greece declared independent of, 92; how freedom from rule of, attained, 94 f.; Great Britain's concern for integrity of, 115, 117, 124

Owning class, *see* Ruling class

"Palace Camarilla," 113

Palmerston, Lord, 115; quoted, 103, 130

Panayotakos, General, 161

Pan-Balkan uprising, dream of, 41

Pangalos, General, 150

Panhellenion, 73, 74, 77; expands jurisdiction of government, 56; replaced by Senate, 74; franchise proposals, 75

Papagos, General, 162, 164

Papanastassiou, 151, 164*n*

Parliamentary system reviewed, 168

Parties, political, 142, 150–53 *passim,* 157, 159, 160*n*, 165, 166, 167; elections and polls, 159, 162, 166

Patriarch of Constantinople, 28, 103

Peloponnesus, the, u n d e r Ottoman rule, 30–33; ruling class attitude toward *Philikè* and the Insurrection, 42 f.; efforts of Ypsilantis to organize, 43, 44 f.; Senate, 44, 45; notables,

Phanariots, 14

Philikè, see Hetairia Philikè

Philippe, Louis, 107

Plastiras, Nicholas, 6, 148, 152, 153, 164, 168, 169

Plebiscite of royalists, degree of control revealed, 162 f.

Political development related to international position, 3, 4 ff.

Politics, Revolution obstructed by preoccupation with, 33

Pollard, A. F., 3

Populist Party, 151, 152, 153, 157, 160*n*, 165; split, 166; Liberal-Populist coalition attempted, 166 f.

Post-war developments, 148–72

Powers, *see* Protecting powers

Preamble (Rhigas), 22*n*

President, constitutional provisions, 51

Primates ("headmen"), 30 ff.

Prokesh-Osten, 105; quoted, 93

Property, private: rights, 21

Property qualification for voting, 26, 78

Proportional representation, 150, 166

Protecting powers, treaty "guarantees" the legal basis for intervention of, 6; by London Treaty offer mediation, 40, 58; ambassadors recognize desire for representative government, 40; recommend tempering monarchy, 41; naval victory at Navarino, 58; part played in creation of new state, 81–95 *passim;* decree hereditary monarchy for new state, 83, 87; attitude toward constitutionalism, 85, 87 ff.; conception of their rôle, 88; selection of monarch, 88, 91, 118–29; powers re choice of sovereign and establishment of regency, 91 f.; loan contracted by, 91, 104, 110, 132; frustrate last Turkish attempt to limit Greek sovereignty, 94; obligations tempered by political interest, 102; attitude toward insurrections, 103, 104, 111, 113; attitude toward constitutional settlement of 1844, 103 ff.; attitude toward Othonian regime, 103 ff., 114 ff.; right to in-

INDEX

Military League, composition of, 137; revolutionary action, 137-39
Ministries, minority or extra-parliamentary, 141
Ministry, dissolution of, 141 f.
Monarchy, foreign policies underlying acceptance of, 4; why selection from native aristocracy deprecated, 14; Korae's opinions, 15, 18; course pursued by Revolution on question of, 37, 38 ff.; selection of ruler by protecting powers, 38, 88, 91, 118-29; first constitutional document envisaging, 40; Capodistrias's stand on, 68 ff., 86; hereditary, decreed by powers, 83; powers avoid commitments re constitutional limitation, 87; rights in respect to constitution, 90; sovereignty transferred from nation to, 90, 92 f.; limited of Otho, 96-110; status as defined by constitutions, 98 ff., 133, 135, 139; constitutional provisions re regency and succession, 107; religion of ruler, 122, 126, 130, 131; conditions laid down by insurrection of 1862, 129; doctrine of national sovereignty, 130, 132; limited democracy of George I, 130-36; identification with state and leadership in international relations, 140, 143; weapon of dissolution, 141 f.; anti-monarchist movement, 149 ff., 6; restoration of, 149, 159 ff. 162; votes cast for, 163; contribution of foreign policy to restoration of, 170; *see also* Alexander; Constantine; George; Otho
Municipal self-government, 28 f., 55, 56
Mylonas, 151

Napoleon I, 25, 35
Napoleon III, 115, 119, 121
National Assembly, *see* National Convention
National Convention, first, 36, 45; constitution framed by, 36, 37, 46 ff.; membership, methods of election to, 53 — second: attempts to remedy mistakes of Constitution, 48 f.; seating of members, 53; constitutional

a compact with nation, 100 f.; decision, 96-110; acquiescence in revolutionary proceedings, 97, 98; Constitution, 93; limited monarchy of, 93; limited monarchy of Greece offered to, 91; first proclamation, 93; limited monarchy of, 93; limited monarchy of Greece offered to, 91; first proclaimed by, 91; hereditary sovereignty of Greece offered to, 91; first proclaimed by, 91; hereditary sovereignty tracted by, 91; hereditary sovereignty of, as King, 89, 90; loan to be contracted by, 91; hereditary sovereignty overthrow of, 5, 102, 115; reasons for overthrow of, 5, 102, 115; reasons for Otho, King, 18, 131, 171; reasons for Orthodox Church
Orthodox Eastern Church, *see* Eastern
Orlandos, J., 48n
Oligarchs, *see* Ruling class
Oldenburg, Duke of, 114
Officers, retirement of, 158; pardons, 165
Nicholas, Czar, 122
Hymn"
etc. (Rhigas) , 20; *see also* "Battle
New Policy of the People of Rumeli,
Negris, Theodore, 55n
Natural rights doctrine, 13, 21, 25, 76
National sovereignty, *see* Sovereignty
National security, European preoccupation with, 3
National security, European preoccupation with, 3
tribution, 66, 78, 88, 90
Turkey, 47n; safeguards, 54; disnational property, transferred by Ottoman system, 9
by Ottoman system, 9
Nationality, preservation of, favored Greek people a basic idea of, 22
to Ottoman Empire, 9; unity of Nationalism, ideology of, 3 f.; menace
156
National Defense movement of 1916, of 1864, 133 ff.
stipulations, 130, 131; Constitution 1863, 129; election of King, 130, 131;
— (of 1862-63) , Decree of Feb. 5, — (of 1843) , Constitution of 1844, 97
— fifth: Constitution framed by, 88 f. 90
elected body, dispersed by soldiery, 70, 73 f.; action by, 86, 89 f.; last
— fourth (July, 1929) , at Argos, 40, matic commission, 82
fected by, 56; instructions to diplomatic commission, 82
tution of 1827, 51 f., 71; revision effected by, 56; instructions to diplomatic
emergency government, 50; Consti- third (1826-27) , 78, 81; sets up
ganization of the provinces," 55 amendment, 54; "law for the or-

183